Beyond Goodbye

Beyond Goodbye

‹◆›

Turning Tragedy into Spirituality

by Dr. Nancy Geller

ARE PRESS

ASSOCIATION FOR
RESEARCH AND
ENLIGHTENMENT

A.R.E Press • Virginia Beach • Virginia

Copyright © 2001
by Dr. Nancy Geller

1st Printing, December 2001

Printed in the U.S.A.

A.R.E. Press
215 67th Street
Virginia Beach, VA 23451-2061

Geller, Nancy, 1962-
 Beyond goodbye : turning tragedy into spirituality / by Nancy Geller.
   p.   cm.
 ISBN 0-87604-431-3 (pbk.)
 1. Consolation (Judaism). 2. Children—Death—Religious aspects—Judaism. 3. Geller, Nancy, 1962—Religion. 4. Parapsychology—Religious aspects. 5. Grief—Religious aspects—Judaism. 6. Bereavement—Religious aspects—Judaism. I. Title.
BM729.C6 G45   2002
296.3'3—dc21

                                      2001006904

Cover design by Lightbourne

To Buddy

Who taught me more about life than anyone

Contents

1

────◆────

The Tragedy Club

The last time I saw my father was the day of his burial. I remember thinking he didn't look like himself as I viewed him in the casket. He was cosmetically enhanced with wild waxy eyebrows he never had in real life. I told him silently that I loved him and would name the child I was carrying after him, a decision finalized at that moment. I then walked into the waiting area, sat down, and within minutes my water broke.

Five hours later I gave birth to our fourth child. Although he was two days early, he was a fairly large baby. After weighing him, the nurse announced, "That's a big ten four," and it was like dad was signing off. I had never attached spiritual importance to anything in my life, but I was struck by these coinciding events. I saw my father for the last time and my son for the first time all in one

day. It simply amazed me that I could say goodbye to
someone I loved my whole life and then meet someone
I'd love for the rest of my life all in the space of five hours.
Perhaps there was more behind things than I'd previously considered.

Soon I was caught up in the sleep-deprived but merry
whirlwind of having a new baby in the house. I didn't
mourn my father excessively because we had been dealing with his imminent death for some time. He had been
seriously ill for months and gravely so weeks before his
passing. Just after he died, I vividly dreamt of him saying
that he was all right repeatedly in a very excited voice. I
didn't think dreams had any bearing on reality, so I paid
it little mind.

We felt renewed by this birth after having been so involved with my father's infirmity and my mother's stroke
the previous year. The new baby was alert and smiled
early on. He was a wonderful addition to our other children, aged five, four, and two. Up until that time, the
youngest child, Roy, was my husband's clear favorite. He
would say that Roy was the epitome of the cute factor.
He was joyful, charming, and irresistibly beautiful. His
eyes were the color of a cornflower blue sapphire set off
by his golden skin tone and blonde hair. Despite all of
this, Roy was different somehow. Quietly independent,
he resisted forming a deep connection to either parent.
There was a look of wisdom in his eyes which was sort of
unusual for a two year old. My husband and I joked that
we treated him like an honored guest in our home, but
secretly we both worried about something happening to
him. It was like we each harbored an irrational yet inex-
plicable fear. I even dreamed that he died, which disturbed me to the point where I shared my concern with
family members. They told me not to worry because
dreams don't mean anything.

On June 12, 1996, lightning struck our home in an unusual way. It came through the wall, forming a punched-out hole in the bedroom closet. It burned and cracked plastic shelving situated by the hole. Six distant connections of shelving revealed similar burn marks as did the carpet. It left a large yellow streak across the closet mirror. The alarm system was destroyed, with pieces of the wall unit strewn about. I thought how dramatic it all looked. Maybe it means something—good luck, possibly? Immediately the thought "No, this is never good luck" entered my mind. My logical response was "then it's nothing because I don't believe in that kind of stuff anyway."

Three weeks later, Roy drowned. The events that led up to this tragedy were so seemingly choreographed, I almost felt I'd been tricked. But, by whom? It was like he had been taken. My husband and I were devastated. We walked through our mutual nightmare reluctantly participating in the drama. For the three days that our son lay in a coma, we somehow knew it was hopeless. Despite our prayers and those of many others, he died. There was a finality in the air all along. We seemed to know that this was our fate and no medicine nor miracle would alter it. My husband now openly admitted that he worried something like this would happen and was not altogether surprised. Neither was I. How could that be if this was sheer accident?

While my son lay in a coma, a doctor pulled my husband aside and confided that his own child had been in an accident and suffered a great deal as a result. All I could think in my state of shock was that his child lived. Why were we discussing it?

I soon realized that we'd been initiated into a secret club. It entitles members to have private knowledge of each other's misfortunes. These were the great and small disappointments our neighbors had experienced that we never knew of, and never would have, if not for our son's death. I called it "The Tragedy Club." So many varied tragic accounts were whispered to us or to our family members that I actually began to look down our street to see if we knew anyone that had not suffered at some point. Just about every family had. It was then that I realized tragedies are not rare exceptions, but rather occur commonly. In fact, intense suffering will be experienced by virtually every individual at some point in his or her life.

I came to welcome this type of commiseration. I was especially touched by letters from people we knew who'd lost a child, but never previously discussed it. They had taken the time to write and it really meant something to me. Along with one sympathy note came the following poem:

> Don't tell me that you understand
> Don't tell me that you know
> Don't tell me that I will survive
> Don't tell me how I will surely grow
>
> Don't tell me that this is just a test
> That I am truly blessed
> That I am chosen for this task,
> Apart from all the rest.
>
> Don't come at me with answers
> That can only come from me,
> Don't tell me how my grief will pass
> That I will soon be free
>
> Don't stand in pious judgment
> In the bonds I must untie
> Don't tell me how to suffer
> And don't tell me how to cry

My life is full of selfishness
My pain is all I see,
But I need you
I need your love, unconditionally

Accept me in my ups and downs
I need someone to share
Just hold my hand and let me cry,
And say "My Friend I Care."

I regret not knowing who wrote this poem, because I had identified with it from the start. It made me aware that a tragedy has certain curious features that are universally experienced. For example, one feels full of selfishness, yet needs to share their grief or the idea that there are answers only the experiencer can work out, suggesting there's more behind things than mere happenstance. I was a little surprised that others would view this as a test or task for growth. Previous to this, I'd never viewed it as a trial of any kind. It was simply the end of everything.

I was overwhelmed by grief compounded by intense guilt. I'd been the parent in charge when the tragedy occurred. The one thought I clung to was perhaps this was part of God's plan. It's difficult to see how a child's death could ever be part of His plan, but I was always aware that my own existence was a result of another child's death.

My mother's life experiences now held new meaning for me. As a young couple, my parents looked forward to starting a family. My mother envisioned having only two children as her sister and brother each had. Their ideas about family were shaped by my grandmother, who frowned on larger broods because she thought they were too draining. Mother eventually gave birth to a girl, followed by a boy a year later. Their family completed, my parents had just begun to enjoy their harmonious home life when tragedy struck. The previously healthy, three-month-old boy died days after a routine vaccination. My mother suffered greatly from this loss. The emotional void created by the death led her to have another child. And another and another. I was the youngest of these, a fifth child she never would have planned if not for the death of her second. I used to tell my mother that I wished such a thing had never happened to her, even if it meant my not being born. I admit that I don't feel that way any more because I'm glad my children got to be born, something that couldn't have happened without my being here.

Knowing these things led me to consider that perhaps it all happens the way it's supposed to. This was how I originally viewed the possible "meant-to-be-ness" of our tragedy. I later came to understand why tragedies occur and their purpose in our lives.

I would never have thought such things could have a purpose. In fact, I never thought my life had a purpose. I just lived it. I grew up with the idea that having somehow found ourselves here, we should do our best. My family seemed fortunate in many ways, and we optimistically assumed that would continue. Bad things only happened to other people. In fact, there was the feeling that if you didn't look their way, the negativity wouldn't affect you. Even though I was sympathetic toward the suffering I encountered as a health professional, it was separate from me.

Now, instead of avoiding the sad side of life, I am immersed in it. I am always ready to hear every aspect of others' misfortunes. I can discuss them endlessly. I feel true compassion for others who are troubled and can easily imagine having their problems. I usually think my situation is worse, but perhaps not. It's as bad as it can be for the experiencer.

In my case, tragedy grabbed hold of me and shook me out of complacency. What resulted was a sort of suspended animation. Things that seemed important in my everyday existence were suddenly meaningless. I may have previously enjoyed the game of life, but no longer wanted to play. Yet, my newly uncluttered mind now possessed a clarity from which answers sprung, making sense out of apparent chaos. My shattered self was reconfigured into a gentler, more compassionate version of the original. No longer invincible, but with an inner strength I never previously had, I came to respect all of Creation and the life process. Although I am keenly aware of my sorrow every day, I appreciate the new way I view life since I've had my eyes forced open. Prior to the loss, I wasn't truly living, or should I say feeling, in some ways. But I'm getting ahead of myself.

2

---<◆>---

The Rabbi Test

It has often been said when confronting hardship that believing in God means one need not question. However, without such belief, there are no answers. My upbringing did not prepare me for the questions I suddenly faced.

I was raised in a nominally Jewish household. We belonged to a conservative temple, but were rarely present at services. I received regular religious instruction at a Hebrew school up until my Bat Mitzvah. After that, I attended synagogue only on high holy days. I always felt like an outsider to "real" observance because somehow I had not done enough. If I could have understood the meaning of the prayers and not just read the Hebrew words, then I would have gotten somewhere. If I continued my instruction or attended services regularly, then I could have been on the inside. If my family had been more observant or ritualistic, then I could've been a contender.

My involvement with organized religion revealed an awesome God who could smile on you or strike you down as He saw fit. It wasn't a loving God who was discussed at school or in our prayers. He was merely portrayed as powerful and solemn. As I grew older, I no longer regretted my family's lack of observance because it was not an inviting experience.

Still, I privately believed in an omnipotent God who knew I was a good person. I occasionally talked and prayed secretly to Him, confident that He could hear. I didn't ask for much, but curiously enough, I always got what I needed. Because of this, I felt on some level that He lovingly watched over me.

This belief was enhanced by occasional thoughts of God that came to me from out of the blue during difficult times in my life. Once as a child, I was confronted head on by two drag racing cars while riding my bicycle down a residential street. There was no way to avoid them so I feared this would be my death. At the last moment, the car directly in front of me stopped short tapping my front wheel. Seconds later as I realized with amazement that I had not been harmed, the thought "God saved you" was practically inserted in my head. I remember thinking it was strange, but nice to know. Another time, as I worriedly waited for my physician to come into the examination room with a test result regarding a potentially serious health problem, I suddenly became aware of the thought "You're going to accept God's will." Although this was a notion alien to my way of thinking at the time, I mentally responded "all right" to the apparent command. In this way I was occasionally aware of God's involvement in my life.

Despite this, I found as I grew older that the people I

respected most did not have much faith in God. There was that private entity they prayed to, but in the real world, one made his own luck. Diseases and misfortunes could be prevented if one carefully avoided the dangers. He was completely in control of his own life with none of the credit nor blame attributed to a higher power. The world was considered random, thus the watchful eye of God or "meant-to-be-ness" of events was relegated to a fable.

The last vestiges of my childhood belief in God were decimated when I learned about the Holocaust. I asked my parents how a righteous God could allow the countless tragedies that took place. The answer was either that He lacked the power to interfere or He didn't really exist. To me, these were one and the same. It saddened me to learn that we probably lived a godless, dangerously random existence that often seemed pointless as well.

My education in science and medicine only served to reinforce this view. It never occurred to me that the scientific method took God out of the equation. Yet, scientifically, anything that can't be proven doesn't exist. It remains theoretical at best. The approach in medicine is similar. Even when controlled studies demonstrate the efficacy of prayer, there is often an intellectual rejection of the data based on the implications.

Such was the personal baggage I carried when I spoke to our rabbi at the funeral parlor. My belief in God was limited, but I assumed his must be great. After all, his whole life was dedicated to religious pursuit. I would draw from his faith and confirm that God still cared. I said to him in a distraught manner, "Rabbi, I accept God's plan," or something to that effect. This compassionate man, searching for the proper response, answered, "God doesn't micromanage these things."

I was blown away by those five words. While the rabbi probably just wanted me to avoid thinking that this was

God's will or some kind of punishment, he could never imagine that his words would launch my spiritual search. I no longer needed to entrust issues of faith to a rabbi because I realized that I had a greater belief in God than he did! His statement referred to the ultimate in a God who made no sense. Here I'm suffering through the most traumatic experience of my life, and my rabbi tells me that God is like some important CEO who's much too busy to be aware of insignificant little me and my problems.

Whatever happened to God is everywhere and knows all? Yearly, on Judgment Day, He decides who shall live and who shall die; so even the rabbi should have assumed that He was involved and this was His will. Instantly, I thought, "The rabbi may have studied for years and be well versed in ritual, but he is no greater authority on God than I am." If God is as awesome as we've repeatedly been told and intuitively know, He would have been aware of our tragedy. He must have heard our prayers while our son lay in a coma and said, "No." Sometimes He says no. To be honest, I wouldn't have minded at that point if it was a punishment because I'd rather have God take an interest in me than be overlooked. Of course, I knew that wasn't the case since He would never let an innocent child down no matter what He thought of me. Ultimately, I came to believe that this was an important and unalterable part of my time here and that's why He said no.

The conviction that God existed and had a role in my life was strengthened by the memory of those almost inserted thoughts described earlier during stressful times. In fact, it occurred again shortly after Roy's death. I would walk around the house lamenting, "I always thought God loved me." An almost external response was, "He does, so figure it out." This was strange in retrospect because I was never told of a loving God. He was awesome, judgmental, wise, punishing, and merciful, but never loving. Yet, here I was certain He loved me despite tragic circumstances. My mission was to find out why this was His will. The explanation was long in coming, but would account for others' tragedies as well.

First, I had to examine my long-held beliefs. Did I really believe in God or was I, in a moment of desperation, just hoping? Was there a divine plan to our lives or were they just the product of random events? I always had a vague understanding that there was an intelligence to the way life evolved and how DNA, the building block of life, replicates (copies). What I really wanted to know was if the God described by the world's religions and wisdom traditions existed. Was there an omniscient, omnipotent, singular Creator who cared for us and whose will was done?

I didn't consider other popular concepts of God such as a Universe that gives back what one puts out, or the idea that we are all really God, yet don't know it. These may in part be true, but standing on their own, our existence still seemed as godless as before.

So what proof *was* there? Was it necessary? Love is a powerful force, yet it is unseen and cannot be proven. In my view, much about our beautiful world could attest to the existence of God. Maybe I should have been considering the brutality and ugliness of our world. Did these attest to the absence of God? If a God dedicated to goodness presided over us, why was there so much adversity?

That's what was nagging at my consciousness. I was not acknowledging a disrespect I had for the God I'd been taught about. He was all powerful, but didn't always lift a hand to alleviate suffering. He created us, had us experience joys and sorrows, and then terminated us. Maybe terminate is a strong word, but we never discussed an afterlife in religious instruction. In fact, we were given the feeling that the soul was some nebulous distillate of the former self that simply basks in the glory of God. Basically, dead was dead. So, with the knowledge that we'd soon cease to exist, it was hard to revere God and even more difficult in the case of a child's death. I then realized something that was not immediately apparent. Belief in an afterlife is essential to a belief in God. How can I say that when many modern religious people *don't* believe in such a thing? First and foremost, a God concept must make sense. If it makes no sense, it won't figure meaningfully in one's view of life. Even with absolute blind faith, an irrational concept will be relegated to the abstract and will be difficult to reconcile with one's day-to-day existence. Simply put, there's an inherent lack of respect for a God who creates us and makes us self-aware, so that we can ultimately cease to exist. Even if you did believe in such a God, you'd wonder if He really cared because He allowed terrible things to happen. Judging from some miserable and short lives, He clearly wouldn't love His children equally. Those who subscribe to "dead is dead" often harbor this disrespect unknowingly. They may feel safe behaving in whatever manner they choose because oblivion awaits them at death.

Thus, belief in God and respect for God depend on the knowledge that one continues on, in my view. Why would anyone care much about God if we were to bloom and die like a rose and get our butts periodically kicked in the process? Our lives would seem pointless or at least extremely unimportant. What would it ultimately matter how you acted or what you accomplished? Religions insist that these are important, based on God's word, but often without stressing a dynamic afterlife. Rigid ideas about heaven and hell are not much better. For the record, there's a wealth of references to *olam habah* (the next world) in holy Jewish texts, but it is often played down because we are supposed to focus on this life.

This is where modern religion has let some of us down and aspiring cults find an opening. The truth of a dynamic afterlife that one has earned a place in gives life meaning and restores respect for God. We would welcome the comfort of an accessible Father. I'm not saying that He should be portrayed as warm and fuzzy, but religion often does not answer this basic human need. The focus is too often on ritual, behavioral guidelines, counseling, or even social engineering. Personally, I don't think religion should be about controlling people. It should be about God and our relationship to Him. More people would follow the tenets of religion if they truly knew God existed and was wonderful.

First, you have to convince some of the clergy. The book *When Bad Things Happen to Good People* is written by a rabbi who concluded after his own tragedy that God has no power to intervene. He describes being struck by how prayer helped people, as though it were something of a mystery to him. He discussed how futile he thought his own prayers would be when members of his congregation requested he pray on their behalf. He's far from the only one with such views. In similar experiences to mine, other bereaved parents have been disappointed by the lukewarm feelings that their clergymen have expressed about an involved God and a real heaven.

Despite this, I was now convinced that a God who made sense was linked to an afterlife, the one thing I hoped was a reality for my son's sake. Unfortunately, I could not simply turn on a belief system. Nothing could have been further from my way of thinking at the time of Roy's death. It would take some pretty remarkable events to change that.

3

———⟨◆⟩———

Out of the Mouths of Babes

A few weeks after Roy's funeral, I had a conversation with my five-year-old daughter that changed the way I viewed death. She came into my room one morning, sat down on the bed, and said, "I want to know about spirits." I was surprised because we had never believed in, let alone discussed such things, nor did our family or friends. In fact, teachers at her preschool told me they purposely avoided discussions about death with her. So I responded, "How do you know that word 'spirit'?" She simply answered, "I know." I then said, "Okay, what's a spirit?" She quickly replied, "Spirits are things that guide you. They're your family. Roy guides me. He guides you."

This shocked me. Although I never thought much about what a spirit was, it sounded right. Suddenly it seemed like I was having a conversation with someone who knew the topic better than I did. But, how could that be? She never heard the words spirit or guide from me because I always thought they sounded creepy and, as concepts, were beyond me. I asked her how she knew. "It comes into my head," she answered. In fact, she thought the informative voice in her head was God. This was yet another topic that was not prominent in our home. She said that Roy died because God wanted him. To think this was the girl who weeks before had wanted to know how her brother could be in heaven in the sky but also buried. She was no longer confused by this and seemed to understand more than I did at this point. I then asked if her information came from anywhere other than what "comes into her head." She said that in her dreams grandpa tells her about where Roy is. "They are together and it's great. It's about love!" She hugged herself as she said this. Then she turned to me suspiciously, "Why are you asking me about this stuff? Don't you know?" I answered that I don't get clear messages like she does. To tell you the truth, I didn't know what to say. She even told me that they loved my husband and were trying to help him. This certainly made sense because he was grieving intensely and, as the ultimate skeptic, had little belief in anything.

When she left the room, I immediately reached for a pen. I wrote down the conversation verbatim because I knew the implications. Without a written account, I might later doubt it took place the way it had. This was perhaps the strongest evidence I'd ever had of the existence of God and an afterlife because it was personal. This was not some fortuneteller who might be trading on my vulnerability with information about a deceased loved one. This was my five-year-old daughter speaking of things that she did not formerly know of and naming her sources. She has always been an honest and serious child, not given to telling stories.

Her credibility is important because she also reported other unusual events. She saw her deceased brother days after he died standing outside my bedroom watching me as I slept. This only occurred twice. He later appeared to her frequently as a "splat" of colors whose thoughts she was aware of and whose laughter she could actually hear. Other young cousins reported this as well. I remember my six-year-old nephew asking his mother if everybody could hear Roy laughing or was it just him?

I had been having some revealing dreams myself as well as possible physical signs, but I didn't take them seriously. At this point I decided I would write such things down and consider their meaning, if any. I wrote how my four-year-old son also had dreams of Roy and my father together "at his new home." He was a little put off because my dad had "black eyes," but comforted because he and Roy were in a "great" place. At first I thought little of his dreams since he was so young. I suppose it was the similarity to his sister's dreams that led me to write about it in my new journal.

My husband teased me about this journal, calling it the "Ethereal Log." I wrote about curious happenings, such as lights, televisions, and clock radios that seemed to turn on and off by themselves, as well as electronic toys that would start talking or playing when I entered the room. Often when this occurred, the children were not home. My husband would try to reproduce the phenomenon without success. Instead of dwelling on these mysteries, I simply wrote them down.

One of the most significant experiences recorded in my journal occurred about six weeks after my son's death. My husband was being treated to one of my rapid fire speeches when I suddenly stopped in the middle of a sentence and stared into space. He asked me what I saw. I told him I wasn't seeing anything. It was what I smelled. Out of nowhere came the overwhelming fragrance of lilacs, causing me to stop speaking, something I never do. I looked around for the source, but in about fifteen seconds it was completely gone. There were no lilacs nor lilac fragrances of any kind in our home that could have been the source for this strange occurrence. My husband did not smell anything, but I knew this was real and somehow directed at me. When I later told my sister about this, she admitted she'd also received a mysterious hit of lilacs recently with no clue as to its origin, as had my mother! Finally, I remembered that my maternal grandmother, who I dearly loved and missed since her death, loved lilacs. It was something I hadn't thought of in years. She would cut a sprig off a lilac bush by the garage, bring it around to each of us for a deep inhalation, and then place it in a vase filled with water on the kitchen table.

A somewhat similar experience occurred weeks later. My husband took me out for dinner to a seaside restaurant. Unfortunately, we argued and wound up driving home in silence. At one point, I became acutely aware of the smell of flowers I couldn't identify. As I wondered what this pleasant fragrance was, the thought "white flowers" entered my mind. I had no idea what that meant. White roses perhaps? "White flowers" again crossed my mind. I was more interested in the source. I looked around our van which was a mess. Clearly, no flowers here. I looked out the closed windows, thinking it might be coming in from the outside. This was unlikely, judging from the neighborhood we were driving through. After arriving home, we called a necessary truce. Now on speaking terms, I told my husband how I smelled something in the van. He looked truly surprised, saying he noticed the same thing "like a damned flower shop" and then suddenly it was gone. Interestingly, we experienced the fragrance at different times during the trip home. I thought it was intended more for him than me, since he received it so strongly and the scent had no meaning for me. I asked him what he thought when he had an experience similar to my lilac episode. Clearly not wanting to be a member of this club, but still a little spooked, he said, "I didn't know. I just kept driving." Incidentally, while shopping I came upon bath products by Sarah Michael with the fragrance of "white flowers." I was surprised that there truly was such a thing. I smelled the products and realized that it was the scent of white flowers, whatever they are, in the van that night. I can't be certain what it means, but at the very least, I wound up with some great bubble bath.

Recording these experiences in a journal turned out to be a good idea. Recent publications on a new area of research called after-death communications (ADCs) reveal that these strange events are actually common among the newly bereaved. In their popular book, *Hello From Heaven*, Bill and Judy Guggenheim describe numerous accounts of these ADCs. Although anecdotal, the similarity of these remarkable experiences reported by credible people seeing, hearing, smelling, feeling, and sensing deceased loved ones, as well as receiving signs from them is a powerful argument for the continued existence of the spirit.

It was my love of bubble bath that led me to the next step in becoming aware of such a continued existence. Shortly after my son died, my sister took me to a local mall in the hopes of temporarily easing my depression. She planned to buy me scented soap and anything else that might improve my mood. We discussed the incidents involving my daughter which impressed her since she knew my little girl well.

My sister wondered how we could find out if the spirit does indeed survive death. She asked me about "that guy" from New York I once told her about. She was referring to an unassuming man from Long Island I'd seen on NBC's *Unsolved Mysteries* who claimed he'd been aware of spirits since surviving a life-threatening illness as a child. He consistently impressed believers and skeptics alike with personal information only their deceased loved ones could know of. Often, the bereaved would find out later that he had been correct about something that, at first, made no sense to them. This all brought great comfort to those suffering loss. He struck me as an honest man, but I didn't know how he could be doing what he said he was.

Now that we had a new interest in such matters, my sister suggested we try to find the book that was written about him. I told her that I couldn't really remember his name, but it was worth a try. We walked into the mall's bookstore and asked where the kook section was. We were promptly led to "New Age." I told her to look for a book on Gary Wayne or Wayne Anderson. She found a book about a psychic medium named George Anderson which had his picture in it. I said, "That's him!" It was entitled *We Don't Die* and was written by Joel Martin and Patricia Romanowski. This amazing account of his talents, and how he became known publicly as "the most tested and reliable psychic medium," is a must read for anyone who is grieving, particularly parents.

Eventually, my sister and I bought additional copies. We gave them to people who had experienced a loss and were hurting. She even bought some for the local hospice. Most found it very comforting. There were two later books written about him as well, *We Are Not Forgotten* and *Our Children Forever*. The latter is also very helpful for grieving parents.

Upon reading these books, one begins to get the idea that we really are here for a reason, that there are no true accidents, and no one is lost to death. I realize the enormity of that statement, but numerous other factors point to this as well. Some of these are described in the next chapter.

I may have been comforted by the above information, but an analytical mind like mine needed to be intellectually satisfied. I proceeded to read hundreds of books ranging from the scientific to the spiritual with the intention of trying to decide what was true, based on logic. Although it was a fascinating journey, the many conflicting opinions I read became confusing. Now that I had the courage to challenge the conventional wisdom, I had to discern which ideas had value. There was a disturbing tendency on the part of many authors to get carried away. After discovering a kernel of truth and sharing it with the reader, they would assume all subsequent thoughts that occurred to them were as poignant and correct as the original. Inevitably, a number would run afoul, leading to questionable conclusions. I don't mind keen speculation, but some authors would promote their ideas as absolute truth, clearly overstepping their bounds. Wading through the spiritual morass is worth it, but only if one is well grounded. Otherwise, there may be a destabilizing effect on one's concept of reality. As the saying goes, "If you don't stand for something, you'll fall for anything."

4

―――――〈◆〉―――――

The Search

I have always considered myself a well-grounded person. Like most people, I experienced life solely through the five senses. My education in science and medicine supported a materialistic, if not agnostic, view of the world. I enjoyed studying math and science because I saw them as pursuits of truth. Mathematics seemed to be an exacting discipline with no annoying gray area. Two and two were four and that was that. Similarly, the aim of science, as I saw it, was to discover the truth behind the way the world works.

Truth has always been very important to me. I could never choose to believe something, no matter how appealing, if I knew deep down that it wasn't true. You could say I have a nose for truth. To illustrate this limited gift, consider the following. As a junior high school student, I watched as our math teacher solved a problem on the blackboard. I raised my hand and stated that it was done incorrectly. He said, 'If you're so smart, why don't you come up here and solve it for the class?" I said, "I don't know how to solve it. I just know what you have up there is wrong." My unenviable ability is recognizing the truth, or more often the lack of it, which enables me to see the problem with someone else's thinking. I do not pretend to have all of life's answers or even any of them worked out completely, but this ability has been a key element in reshaping a reasonable framework of reality from my recent experiences and study. While it is difficult to deal with such intangible subjects as God or an afterlife, I believe my search has led to a wider view of reality that is at least rooted in truth, if not wholly accurate.

My personal search for the answers to these age-old questions began with finding out the views of the scientists I most admired: Newton, Edison, and Einstein. The opinions that these great minds held of God's existence, the meaning of life, and consciousness and its survival after physical death would certainly influence me. After all, these men were all geniuses in their own right whose work served to explain the natural laws of the physical world. Einstein's theories, Edison's inventions, and Newton's mechanical model of gravitation all did not take God or any nonphysical forces into account. Their work was that which agnostic scientific devotees would later rest their reality on. Yet, these famous critical thinkers were not agnostics themselves. In fact, the older they became, the more they believed in God and spiritual existence. As scientists, one might assume the opposite would be true, but it's not.

This information was not exactly in the mainstream. It had to be teased out of biographical accounts. It is a little known fact that Edison tried to construct a machine that would allow spirit communication between the dead and the living. He openly discussed his views on the survival of the personality after death and the desire for communication in the October 30, 1920 issue of *Scientific American*. Newton's fascination with alchemy in his later life was clearly an attempt to factor the metaphysical into his scientific pursuit. However, Einstein's evolution in thinking on such matters is perhaps the most typical of a scientist who does not wish to look at anything metaphysical but will not ignore truth. As a child, he received religious instruction but then turned away from it as a nonobservant Jew. Early in his career, he rejected the notion of an afterlife or a God with a will like ours. As his life and work unfolded, he found himself a "deeply religious man" in the sense that "cosmic religious feeling is the strongest and noblest motive for scientific research" as he put it. He once wrote, "Everyone who is seriously involved in the pursuit of science becomes convinced that a Spirit is manifest in the Laws of the Universe – a Spirit vastly superior to that of man, and one in the face of which we, with our modest powers, must feel humble."

Knowing that great scientists had come to these types of conclusions allowed me to keep an open mind. The next step would be to take a good look at unexplained phenomena that had impressed me years ago when first exposed to them. I filed these curious items away in my mind with a plan to one day take a closer look at their significance. Well, the day had come. These would include the remarkable abilities of George Anderson, the life story of Edgar Cayce, near-death experiences, Kirlian photography, the government's remote viewing program, and numerous examples of parts of living systems having information of the whole.

One of the most impressive of the above was Kirlian photography. I first saw this demonstrated on an old television show hosted by Leonard Nimoy called *In*

Search Of. A Russian couple developed a type of photography using a generator to create high frequency electrical fields. The resultant photographs depicted a form of radiation emanating from living things that revealed a dynamic structural patterning not seen with inorganic (nonliving) samples. What I found amazing at the time was a leaf photographed before and after cutting off the tip resulted in the same detailed image of the entire leaf. How could there be a complete leaf photograph when a good size piece was cut off? It seemed to be that an energy double that remained intact was caught on film in some way. A physical section of the leaf could be removed, but the apparent energy blueprint remained whole and present. As animals and humans were shown on Kirlian photography to have similar emanations, I concluded that there was probably an indestructible energy behind living things with untold ramifications. I filed this thought away at the time, but now I wanted to read about it. Some felt these emanations or energy fields or energy bodies represented the aura or spiritual aspect long described by mystics and depicted by artists. Valerie Hunt, a muscle physiologist, makes a convincing case in her book *Infinite Mind* that the human aura or electromagnetic field is measurable with reproducible results. In any event, Kirlian photography revealed changes in the patterning of emanations in areas where disease would later develop, attesting to the likelihood that the energy body (or energy aspect) is a blueprint that directs the physical manifestation.

Another impressive television demonstration involved a Chicago bellhop named Ted Serios. This man could mentally focus on something he'd seen, such as a building, touch a camera, and make that image appear on the film. In fact, in one instance the photographic image revealed an incorrect number of windows because his memory of how it looked was imperfect. This remarkable ability suggested to me the idea that thoughts truly are things. It's one thing to have an image projected on your retina and quite another to conceive one from your memory and transfer your thought to film. Serios was not the only person with this ability. Eastman Kodak Laboratories have in the past exhibited such photographs under the label "thought photography." This was another of those curiosities I had mentally filed away but now wished to research further.

I remembered another time while flipping through television channels, I caught an exchange between a "skeptic" and a near-death experiencer on a daytime talk show. It was only moments that I remained on the station, but the demeanor of this man struck me. He insisted he didn't care what anyone thought of him. Only he knew what had happened during his near-death experience, and since then he was driven to help the dying by working with hospice patients. There was something so uncommonly honest about this man that I paused to note his name, Dannion Brinkley, and commit it to memory. Years later, I came upon the book he wrote, *Saved by the Light.* Due to my earlier impression of him, I purchased it and was taken with what seemed to be an embarrassingly honest and straightforward account of what he experienced.

Near-death experiences were another subject I planned to eventually examine. My interest heightened when Dr. Melvin Morse came on the scene. He reported that a number of his pediatric patients, obviously a culturally unpolluted group, described experiences similar to those of adults. The consistent elements such as leaving one's body, entering a tunnel, encountering an appealing brightness, and beings of light were impressive coming from the mouths of babes. Some of these youngsters had not been taught about God or religion. Ironically, when I saw an interview with Dr. Morse some time later saying that predeath visions, near-death experiences, and post-death visitations are all events dealing with the same realm (where we go when we die), the skeptic in me reflexively said, "Oh no! The kooks got to that nice, credible doctor and he's one of them now!" That's where I was coming from. I was unknowingly biased against such a concept because I'd never taken a serious look at it. Without having done the homework, I sat in judgment. Today I'm inclined to agree with Dr. Morse. I enthusiastically recommend his books, *Closer to the Light* and *Parting Visions.*

Perhaps the most impressive material which supports these ideas as well as an omniscient and loving God is the collection of thousands of documented readings by Edgar Cayce. In my view, the "sleeping prophet," as he was known, is in a class by himself. This unassuming, uneducated man could accurately diagnose illness and describe effective treatment plans all from a sleep state. He would use medical terms that he did not know consciously, speak foreign languages he never learned, and report other information regarding distant places and events. Upon awakening, he would have no knowledge of what he'd revealed and was at times disturbed when he found out that others had taken advantage of him while he was in trance. Interestingly, I found his autobiography by Thomas Sugrue to be most impressive for its depiction of his deep humility and integrity as opposed to his psychic abilities. In today's world of disintegrating values, its hard to imagine anyone having these qualities to such a degree. They are likely a result of his abiding faith. A devout Christian, Cayce read the Bible cover to cover repeatedly and enjoyed teaching Sunday school. He initially resisted the references to reincarnation that came up in his own readings because of traditional religious beliefs. Despite this, the Cayce readings reveal the human lifetime to be a brief interlude of learning in an ongoing odyssey of the soul through space and time with the experiences of the personality, a temporary role, absorbed at death by the true self, a cosmic being. The life story of Edgar Cayce is so powerful in all of its ramifications that even today, when I'm considering a new concept, I'll refer to the Cayce material to decide if it has merit.

Where does science fit into all of these apparently supernatural ideas? Anyone who has heard the term "quantum" is probably aware that our view of reality is already being redefined scientifically. Such issues are neatly handled in Michael Talbot's *The Holographic Universe*. Two of these were especially meaningful to me. The first dealt with the nature of holograms and how they may apply to the way the mind works. What I found more interesting than its application was the basic properties of a hologram. When holographic film is broken into two pieces, each will generate a complete hologram of the original object, when the proper laser is applied, instead of just a section, as one would expect. This continues to be the case when there are several broken pieces. Each piece will generate a smaller but complete version of the original. This suggests that even the smallest bits of film have information of the whole. This concept of pieces having information of the whole is also seen in living things. By way of its nuclear DNA, each cell of an organism has information of the whole. This has always suggested a divine design to me.

The other point the author made that was particularly meaningful for me dealt with consciousness. The following question was asked. Where is one's consciousness when he is a character in his own dream? Is it in the head of the character or all around him because the action is occurring in the dreamer's head? Instinctively, I felt *both* and who knows where else? This highlights a greater potential of the human mind than we usually consider. The mind, meaning our personality and memory, is apparently not the brain, but a consciousness with vast potential. It always disturbs me when this potential is described in finite terms such as the common complaint "we only use a fraction of our brains." To me, the brain is a well-differentiated lump of tissue capable of accommodating the mind (or energy-consciousness) which it needs for expression, i.e., to function in the physical world. Thus, in my view, the brain would be similar to a computer that, while sophisticated, is nothing without the software.

Consciousness appears to operate on a number of levels and sometimes in more than one location as evidenced by out-of-body experiences. These have been described since time immemorial and are an important part of the near-death experience but up until recently considered an unproven phenomenon. I feel Dr. Michael Sabom has made a serious case for out-of-body experiences by conducting a study of patients whose hearts had stopped. The cardiologist compared the accounts of patients in an arrest situation who reported being out of body with guesswork by patients in a similar circumstance who had not. The results were impressive. Those who reported being out of body may well have been. This unusual phenomenon is also a proposed mechanism for remote viewing.

Our government actually funded a program whereby participants used psychic ability to view remote sites. Information gained from remote viewing of distant locations and activities was to be used for intelligence gathering, but the yield was not what they had hoped for. To me, it's not important that remote viewing did not meet their expectations, but that it worked amazingly well sometimes. It appears to be another testament to the fact that consciousness is not limited to the brain alone.

Before I took a serious look at these types of subjects, I never realized how closed minded I was. I considered myself purely conventional. Today, I don't comment on any discipline, philosophy, movement, or religion unless I've done my homework first. I remember some of my family were taken aback when I read the New Testament, as well as other religious texts. I told them that I wasn't considering converting but had simply realized that I had to educate myself and not blindly adopt another's perception. Only then could I legitimately opine and comment on such subjects. I recommended that they do the same. Needless to say, I'm still waiting.

In any event, looking into these mysteries made me aware that there is more to our physical world than meets the eye. The possibility of the spirit or energy-consciousness surviving physical death suggests we have a purpose here. We aren't just twiddling our thumbs. Our choices and behavior may really matter. We take our life experiences and acquired wisdom and continue on. While this makes more sense than a death where we cease to exist, it actually took some personal experiences and a revelation or two to finally convince me. It should be noted that many people cannot widen their view of reality unless they have some type of psychic or mystical experience themselves. They need some personal knowledge of the unseen to make that leap. While I understand this may be needed to change long held views, I regret that the door is closed for them. The good news is that simply keeping a more open mind increases the likelihood of having a meaningful personal experience. It amounts to a heightened awareness. As the saying goes, "You'll see it when you believe it."

5

————— ⟨◆⟩ —————

Revelation

It would be nice if one could simply choose to believe in a higher power or a spiritual realm. It would be even better if they could choose to be more compassionate. Unfortunately, it's not that easy. Some new age books suggest it is, but a premeditated adoption of a sweetness and light attitude does not change one on the inside. Meaningful experiences are usually required for such fundamental change. I think that's part of the reason we're here. It must take living through a difficult earthly experience to change the complexion of one's soul. At least that's how one woman who'd been raped viewed it.

Personal experiences which convince one of a Higher Power can be dramatic like a mystical vision or more subtle like feeling a presence or a spiritual touch or scent. These events, however small, are important because they force one to incorporate things unseen, yet substantive, into their framework of reality. It's easy to believe the sound from a dog whistle is real but imperceptible. Yet, it's difficult to imagine the multitude of other phenomena that are real but imperceptible. We resist even trying because of their intangible nature.

I was intellectually persuaded by the exhaustive search touched on in the last chapter, but it wasn't enough. It would take a personal revelation to own a belief in God and spiritual existence. This occurred on my birthday following Roy's death. After returning from a family lunch marking a most unhappy birthday, I withdrew to a rear bedroom to take a nap. Upon awakening, I kept my eyes closed and marveled at hearing chimes consisting of three tones. We owned no chimes and no television sets were on. Besides, these had a rhythmic nature as opposed to wind driven. I soon realized they occurred only when I exhaled. I found it very interesting that these could be sounds confined to my mind alone. To be certain of this, I breathed out slowly and the tones sort of stretched out. Then I sped up my breathing and the chimes sped up. In addition there was a sort of celestial music in the background which I didn't particularly like. Did something break in my head and forever more I'd now hear these sounds? Was that a slight exposure to another realm while I was in an altered state or just a dream-type phenomenon? In any event, an alarm buzzer was ruining this experience so I decided to get up and shut it off. Why it was going off in the late afternoon when no one had set it, I didn't know. I opened my eyes, sat up, and the chimes ceased. I shut off the alarm and smiled as I noticed the clock read 6:12 p.m. That was the time Roy was born, 6:12 on 12/6. I told myself not to get carried away with nonsense, but it got me wondering. Could the lilac and white flower scents experienced by more than one person at different times and places truly have been sent from elsewhere, like the world of spirit? Much of what I'd read suggested this was possible. Was my daughter right all along? I walked to the living room, sat down on the couch, and looked out the window. The view was obstructed by partially closed blinds. The idea of anything beyond the touch-and-feel concrete world seemed fantastic in relation to my everyday existence.

Then I had a revelation. It was the only one I've ever had. The thought practically hit me on the head. If we are here for some learning experience of the soul, what kind of workshop or testing ground would an inconceivably awesome God make? A cut-and-paste construct that let you know you were in a game-type environment, or something so real that you couldn't tell there was anything else? The vertical blinds I was staring at seemed to glow with the power of this thought. Why hadn't I ever taken such an idea seriously before? The biases I previously held against such thinking were almost silly knee-jerk assumptions, but nevertheless pervasive. I'm reluctant to admit these involved size, numbers, garbage, and decadence. I'd rather not elaborate.

O.K., if you insist. I could handle the difference in size between man and insects and, to a lesser extent, microorganisms, but not when I thought how small he looked on the ground when I'd taken off in an airplane. I mean, man was so small in relation to the planets, stars, and the vastness of the cosmos, he seemed way too small to be divine. The sheer *number* of humans seemed to make divinity impossible. There were billions of us, let alone all of the other organic and inorganic matter God would have to concentrate on. It was too much for me to conceive of. Also, I always thought that the incredible beauty of some man-made creations suggested we may be something special; but on the other hand, we also generated so much garbage, too much to be divine. All of the decadence in the world was a testament to me that we definitely weren't. I had simply been thinking too small. It was ridiculous for me to impose my limitations on an inconceivable God. Yet, I'd done so for much of my life without really thinking about it. I never consciously examined these notions. They just played in the background.

When such mindless assumptions go unexamined, they often serve as a basis for lack of faith. For example, there's a common sentiment that there can't be a God in a world with so much suffering. It's an unspoken, unexamined absolute that maintains entrenched agnosticism. If one doesn't consciously settle the irreconcilable aspects of his faith such as "God cares, but doesn't answer my prayers," then it won't be real for him. At least, his faith won't be relevant to his daily life because on some level, he's logically concluded that God doesn't care or doesn't exist. He is inaccessible or has chosen to deny him. All of these possibilities are worthy of turning away from, and unknowingly, that's exactly what happens. Thus, it's unscrutinized, unarticulated assumptions that result in the godless perspective many people operate from.

The simple act of openly stating such assumptions or writing them down goes a long way in thinking them through. They may seem silly like some of mine or profound like questioning God's role in brutality. Some individuals confounded by such questions and unsatisfied by the answers given in childhood become atheists. I think they'd rather simply conclude that there's no God than consider the ominous alternative: The omnipotent Creator exists and is responsible for all of His creation including its inevitable sequelae of evil and other bad outcomes. A distaste for negativity stops us from considering such a thing and we, in effect, arbitrarily limit what God will tolerate.

In the Talmud, the oral tradition of the Hebrew Bible or Torah, God states that He has created the evil inclination and He has created Torah as its antidote. If one involves himself in Torah, he will not be delivered into its hand. Kabbalist David Sheinkin put forth a similar idea in his book, *Path of the Kabbalah.* He stated that evil is created from fallen good. Jewish mystics see man's role on earth and the task of humanity as a whole as taking evil, which is really broken shards of good, and, through our actions and way of life, elevating it back to the source of good. In fact, in the Bible, God is known to send Hebrew armies to fight one wicked group or another. No matter how you look at it, they were still going to kill people, let alone the wicked individuals of Noah's time or of Sodom and Gomorrah that He was going to take care of personally. We are told on the High Holy days that we are written in His Book of Life and that fates are decided as to who shall live, die, suffer, go hungry, wax rich, be poor, and the like. The point is made that He is on top of all of this and clearly in control. If, as millions of near-death experiencers have reported, we do go to a beautiful spiritual realm or heaven when we die, then suffering and tragic deaths would be seen in a different perspective. These would have meaning as opposed to being meaningless. I know it sounds heartless, but perhaps it's true that the improved individual one becomes as a result of this devastation could not be achieved with a lesser experience. This doesn't mean a child dies for our learning. They continue on their own spiritual path in another realm after having played a part in our growth.

This, to me, is the straightforward answer as to why some people experience miracles or "guardian angel" protection, and others in similar situations don't. Even the latter group will admit to having, at some time in their lives, benefited from unseen "help" or Providence. What about these accounts of angels or spiritual beings intervening so that tragedies are prevented? They are too numerous to discount unless you think everyone is lying or deluded. I don't. They often involve a commanding voice or the sensation of a physical hand pushing or pulling, depressing a car's brake or accelerator pedal, or leading one out of a fire. My personal favorite occurred in the early 1950s in Beatrice, Nebraska, when the West Side Baptist Church sustained a natural gas explosion as a result of a leaky pipe, three minutes before choir practice. None of the fifteen choir members were present because for the first time in one hundred years all were late. Coming from different locations, each had a different reason for being detained! Even I experienced a similar divine hand when I was in my first year of medical school, although I didn't see it that way at the time. I left early one morning for classes and hadn't driven very far when my car was struck by another motorist, who was apparently intoxicated. The car was propelled on to someone's property and headed straight for their closed garage door. A few moments after I stopped operating the controls, I became aware of another of those rare inserted thoughts, "Put your foot on the brake." I wouldn't heed this, however, because I assumed it was too late and what good would that do as I was already crashing into the garage door. Again, an undeniable command, "Put your foot on the brake!" led to my braking as I mindlessly obeyed. The car stopped a few feet short of the back wall of the garage which happened to be empty. Why was I guided toward a safe outcome in that instance, but not ten years later? Why are some tragedies prevented and others permitted? Are some angels asleep at the wheel? If there truly is divine intervention, it has to make sense. The obvious answer is that these forces are aware that the awful thing is to go down. It's not supposed to be prevented. Protective spiritual forces may even be at work, making sure it goes down as intended. I definitely felt a choreographed nature to our tragedy. It was as though everything went perfectly wrong at the same time. We often hear of a tragedy where several things have to go wrong for it to occur, and I believe that's no accident.

It should be evident that I have ventured forth into the uncomfortable territory of God's role in negativity and emerge convinced that despite this, He is inherently good and in control. I'm not just taking the word of some near-death experiencers who attest to this. I feel we are endowed by our Creator with an appreciation of beauty, truth, love, and justice because these good things are important to Him. It is in this way we re made in His image. In fact, He tells us of His goodness and omnipotence in the inspired word of the holy texts of the world's religions and wisdom traditions. I believe these are all different paths to God that He had a hand in bringing forth. The different religions each serve respective followers in a way that's right for where they are spiritually. It's no accident what situation one is born into. To me, the religions are like different costumes or languages with which we approach God. And like everything else, they're not perfect. Your costume may not necessarily fit well. You may see a lot wrong with others' costumes. You may think yours is the best or the only one that's real. Why doesn't everyone wear one like yours? Maybe you don't like any of them. I believe these costumes, or more correctly, symbolic languages, are the reason people of different religions see different deities when they have a mystical vision or a near-death experience. What they are experiencing is simply being couched in their terms or communicated in their language.

In any event, that simple revelation I had obviously went a long way in my attaining a belief in God. It's truly a wonderful thing. Once I had it, nothing looked the same. Every person, object, and process gained greater

stature in this more meaningful context. I felt raised up
and humbled at the same time. Suddenly, God's handi-
work seemed obvious where I'd resisted it before. It was
in vivid rainbows, which were a fascination no longer to
be reduced to simply a scientific phenomenon. It was in
my children's faces, no longer reduced to millions of
years of evolutionary trial and error. It was in the eerie
way my infant son quickly turned into a toddler with a
striking resemblance to Roy. People often apologized for
mistaking them, but I was never dismayed because I saw
God in it. On one hand, I was experiencing a year of intense grief. On the other, I was falling in love with an en-
gaging new baby who looked and acted very much like
his brother. Sometimes, I felt like crying out, "Roy, where
have you gone?" and then this blond kid with a similar
face would run by and I'd think, "Wait, who's that again?"
It was a confusing time, but God's role in it was obvious
to me. Those who have experienced meaningful coincidences may know what I mean. I had begun to understand the way in which He works. We can't know it all,
but we're probably supposed to appreciate some of it.
Alas, this profundity is lost on the world's concrete thinkers. My husband's take on the similarity of our sons is
simply, "He comes, he goes. I don't get it."

6

—— ❬◆❭ ——

The Poor Man's
Near-Death Experience

I consider the near-death experience (NDE) to be of great importance in understanding the spiritual origin and context of our lives. NDEs are fascinating accounts of individuals who, at the moment of physical death, move through a tunnel toward a beautiful light. They meet spiritual beings, review their lives, and return with information they should have no way of knowing. While they have been described throughout history, millions more have been reported worldwide since the physician-author Dr. Raymond Moody first coined the term in the seventies. Mally Cox-Chapman, the Yale-educated author who wrote *The Case for Heaven*, likened the numerous reports of NDEs to millions of telegrams sent to inform us that there's a heaven.

For me, their importance lies in how much information we gain about human existence. They expose a tangible afterlife, the likelihood of a Higher Power, and a glimpse into the way it all works. For instance, we know these experiences occur when patients have no vital signs establishing a type of living at death. Leaving the body attests to there being a spiritual element to humans separate from the physical. Instead of just hanging "out there," they are met by spiritual beings such as deceased relatives or angels which not only suggest a Higher Power, but a hierarchy or order to the cosmos. They review their lives, feeling appropriate pride or shame as though going over their performance in some learning experience. Finally, they are often told they must return to finish their work, suggesting one comes to earth with a purpose and leaves at an appointed time. The whole NDE phenomenon supports a God-involved, somewhat controlled human experience as opposed to a random mess. Reports of NDEs are also comforting in their descriptions of a beautiful heaven and mostly positive experiences at death. Other spiritual experiences may tell us there's more to life than just the physical world, but none spell out what we're doing here like the NDE.

I've heard scientists argue that these experiences are the result of a dying brain. They blame the hypoxia, or deprivation of oxygen, as the cause. The problem with that theory? NDEs have been reported by those who thought they were at the point of death but actually weren't. Thus, no decreased oxygen had occurred. For example, in one case, an individual was certain he was about to be hit by a car. At the last moment, he wasn't. How do scientists counter this? They don't. They would probably request the details of each such case and seek to cast doubt on them. So what if they impugn the character of some near-death experiencers? A small price to pay to preserve their precious theories and comfortable belief system. In their defense, I would grant they have not read the numerous, detailed NDE accounts reported by children and reputable adults of all races, all walks of life, and varied geographical locations. Many reports are extremely credible, but it's not in the scientists' interest to study them. It takes a lot of time. You can assume with their busy lives, these skeptics are not spending hours open-mindedly poring over reports of NDEs when they never had much respect for their merits in the first place. So, we can assume they've never really seen most of the material.

It's what's in these accounts, the rich detail, that's so persuasive. Possibly the strongest evidence of the reality of NDEs is their transformative nature. Experiencers feel certain it's real. They're comforted by the love that awaits them. They've become aware of a true spiritual context to their lives. Convinced that existence has a purpose, their approach to living often changes. Previously suggestible lay people now have conviction and cannot be dissuaded by doubting doctors and scientists. Their certainty can even weaken the doctor-patient relationship because they know something the doctor doesn't. So what else is he wrong about? Sometimes I think the faith we put in science and medicine today makes professionals in these fields seem like the high priests of our time. They appear to view *themselves* this way or at least view their work as a kind of religious doctrine. I've seen them defend their beliefs, which are at best theoretical, with almost religious fervor. What disturbs me is the notion that what millions experience as real can be written off as lies, delusion, or imagination. I've always tried to give people more credit than that.

Dr. Raymond Moody, the pioneer NDE researcher, described in his book *Life After Life* how some professionals were skeptical because they had treated patients for years without ever hearing of such an experience firsthand. He told them that patients often consider this to be very personal and were unlikely to volunteer the information. He suggested they ask patients who had survived a cardiac arrest if they remembered anything of the experience. This struck a chord with me. I was one of those physicians who'd been involved with clinically dead patients and had never heard such an account. The idea that no one discussed it because it was personal, like their sex lives, made sense but was also very convenient for NDE proponents. I decided I would try asking next time.

The first person I approached was a young woman whose heart stopped beating following a motorcycle accident. I fully expected her to say she remembered nothing while being resuscitated. I was amazed when she answered in almost a whisper, "I've never told this to anyone, but since you asked…" She then went on to say she went out of her body, rose above the scene, and was actually looking down on the rescue effort. No longer feeling any pain, she became aware of a "presence" she was supposed to go with. She was making a case to this being that she couldn't leave her small children because they needed her. There was no one else to care for them. Suddenly, she was back in her body and again experiencing intense pain from her injuries.

My next inquiry involved a middle-aged man who had suffered a cardiac arrest following a respiratory arrest. Again the response, "Funny you should ask … " This fellow left his body and viewed the resuscitation from a number of vantage points. His consciousness was not limited in the way he was ordinarily used to. He found he no longer had difficulty breathing and was finally comfortable but was concerned about leaving loved ones. He soon returned to his body and its physical struggle.

This was incredible—randomly chosen individuals I'd

come in contact with describing similar accounts as those found in books about near-death experiences! I'd given them no encouragement and offered no information myself. I simply listened silently to these NDEs which, I must be honest, are much more convincing when you hear them firsthand.

I'm impressed by the ramifications of such experiences. They seem to say something important about humanity. The fact that one doesn't simply wander around out of body, but instead meets with a loving spiritual being on the way to a destination suggests order, not randomness. The importance of love and truth is heartening. The life review suggests it really does matter what we do, and even think, while on earth. The meetings with deceased relatives suggests that no human being is lost to death and that, in itself, is awesome. Remarkably, there are reports of friends or relatives encountered during NDEs who experiencers thought were living but were actually dead. There are accounts of servicemen, arising after losing consciousness in a combat situation, stating they knew who died and who survived the battle before being told. They had been with their compatriots during an NDE and knew who would not be returning. Experiencers often report being aware of God or a Creator. Even atheists have returned from NDEs with an awareness of a Creative Intelligence.

One of the things I find to be of great interest is the strong conviction of near-death experiencers. Often their perspective changes, which results in a completely different life with different aims. This transformation is unlikely to result from a sham experience. At the start of this process, I viewed this topic with a healthy skepticism, but unlike other skeptics, I'm not stingy with the benefit of the doubt. It literally makes more sense for these to be real than for them not to be. And I'm not afraid to envision a world or larger Reality that is loving, ordered, awesome, and downright divine.

While I've never had an NDE myself, I have had what I call "the poor man's near-death experience." It was not in the cards for me to approach the threshold of my own death, encountering light and love, only to heroically return to the joyous arms of loved ones. No, the death I was near was my son's. There was no return. There was no light. There was only finality and darkness. Still, it was obvious from the beginning that this was a transformative experience. Curiously, as I sat in shock in the emergency room waiting for word on my son's condition, I didn't ruminate about events of the day. Instead, I kept repeating that I had always judged others too harshly and how I'd never want to be judged by me. Despite other vital concerns, this was what I uttered over and over again. It was all I could think about. In retrospect, it really doesn't make any sense. However, it was all-important to some part of me. Whether or not this was a life lesson about compassion and humility that I was supposed to learn, I am forever changed in this respect. I don't judge others harshly anymore. I understand why people do what they do. I don't always approve of it. I still think ethical and moral behavior is very important, but I view it in a "we're all struggling in this together" spirit. I definitely feel greater compassion for others. This fundamental change was accompanied by other changes that near-death experiencers report as well. These mutual sequelae include gaining greater clarity, becoming less materialistic, completely losing the fear of death, being more spontaneous, and oddly, having an enhanced sense of humor. The latter is especially true with regard to myself. I simply don't take myself all that seriously anymore. It's a relief, really.

From the start, there was an instant clarity about who I was and what I wanted in life. It was just *there*. I would no longer be affected by others' expectations, nor overly concerned with what they thought. While this may sound optimistic on the surface, I actually didn't care if I lived or died. Previously, I'd been very fearful of death, but that was no longer the case. If my two year old could do it, I certainly could. What was so important about my life, anyway? Tragedies definitely change one's perspective. Although I came to believe the spirit survives death, the idea of my own death no longer bothered me, either way.

My previous fear of death made me cling to life so tightly that I lived very cautiously. This, coupled with a lack of faith where only I was in control of my fate, translated into a fear of living. Something could always go dreadfully wrong if I wasn't careful. This fear and many others were lost as a result of the tragedy and finding out that God is real and involved in my life. I'm no longer preoccupied with past concerns, nor fretting about the future. I still have goals and hope all turns out well, but no matter what, I'm okay. This is what God has given me. For the first time, I'm living in the present and smelling the roses along the way. That's a big deal because I used to live concerned only with the future and holding my breath all the time. I don't take life so seriously anymore. I see the humor in many things I never had before. Most important, I'm more peaceful and accepting of life as it comes.

Through excoriating conditions, I've been relieved of whatever pedestal I was afraid to fall from. Now I'm spontaneous instead of having everything carefully orchestrated. The perfectionist trip has clearly ended. In fact, I'm much less materialistic. This doesn't mean I don't appreciate material things. I still enjoy them and consider their acquisition a way to treat myself. It instills that I'm a deserving person, as an unconditionally loving parent would view me; the way God does. I can just see people who know me saying, "What's she talking about? She's still materialistic, and judgmental, too!" It's true, I'm still the same person playing the same role as I did before. It's how I view things that's different. Material things are no longer that important. They don't define me or increase my worth. They don't enslave me. If I had to, I could leave it all without much regret.

These transformative changes all stem from a loosened grip on life. In the aftermath of being "near death," I no longer clutch at life. I still have the same day-to-day concerns, but I can't help viewing them as an observer as well as a participant. I sometimes also view my own thoughts and actions in this way. Confusing new responsibilities abound. My spiritual search spawned concerns about the general quality of my consciousness as well as my attitude. These days, I try to behave in a way that reflects the kind of person I want to be. My view before may have been dim, but at least it was simple. Now I find myself inadvertently dissecting all of my feelings and actions as I go through the day. I suppose this dizzying self-evaluation is part of living a spiritual life, but it often seems very obnoxious.

I believe my poor man's near-death experience has similar sequelae to the classic NDE because both involve a shaking out of complacency, stunning revelations, and a change in one's priorities due to a new definition of what our lives truly are. It seems these changes come from confronting loss of life, whether it be during a heavenly NDE or a hellish poor man's NDE. There is a partial loosening of the spirit from the physical which forever changes the experiencer. It's like living with one foot in this world and one in another.

7

—————〈◆〉—————

There's a Prebirth Experience, Really?

I consider near-death experiences to be exactly what the countless credible experiencers say they are, real events. Logically, I would take their implications seriously as well. Sometimes, however, an account may be hard to believe due to its content or the fact that the experiencer could not prove they were clinically dead at the time. Such was the case with Betty Eadie. Ironically, hers is one of the most well-known near-death experiences. In her best-selling book, *Embraced by the Light*, she described her visit to a heavenly realm. Among the wondrous phenomena she encountered was spirits waiting to be born. Their minds were not blank slates. Instead, they were thinking beings anticipating planned incarnations on earth. They each had their mission as well as lessons to learn. When I first read about this, it was just another element in a mind-boggling story that I simply filed away. However, she's not the only near-death experiencer to report this. There are others.

I soon came upon a book detailing the initial research into something called the prebirth experience (PBE). PBEs are experiences where individuals, usually mothers, have some form of contact with a soon-to-be-born child. While not the first to describe such incidents, the author, Sarah Hinze, makes an impressive case in *Coming from the Light* for PBEs to be taken seriously. She has given birth to nine children, as well as mothering nine foster daughters and a Laotian family of eight. Her pursuit of this subject began after she experienced it herself. Remarkably, she was told in "announcing dreams" by a number of her preborn children that it was their time to come to earth and she was to be their mother. Aware that near-death experiencers had sometimes reported seeing people on the other side waiting to be born, she sought evidence for life before life. I thought, "There's a prebirth experience, really?" After reading the collection of true stories contained in the book, however, I don't see how one doesn't realize there's something to this. In one account, a woman dying from being burned in a plane crash had an NDE in which she decides she does not wish to return to life. She then meets her as-yet-unborn son who is distressed that he will not be born to her and cannot perform his mission. I later saw this woman on television giving the same account. She seemed unconcerned by the scarring left by her wounds. Her candor was impressive as she described how she has since given birth to this child, even naming him what he called himself on the other side.

The author noted the different countries in which the prebirth experiences had occurred and hypothesized that the phenomenon is universal. That is to say, it's a good bet that like the near-death experience, it occurs in all races and cultures. Of the cases described 63 percent were witnessed by the mother-to-be, 13 percent by the father-to-be, and 24 percent by others, including siblings, other relatives, close friends, and midwives.

In another account from *Coming from the Light,* a woman named Audrey, who never thought she'd have a spiritual experience, wound up having several PBEs, starting just prior to the birth of her second child. Unlike the first delivery, she was given an anesthetic gas causing her to go "in and out." While under, a man dressed in white stood next to her shoulder and explained how spirits got their bodies. She could see five forms a distance away, two of which were fairly close. Apparently the forms represented spirits coming to get their bodies. A roaring sound that came in rushes coincided with the forms moving closer. When the nearest form got right next to her, she came to and delivered. Twelve months later, she was delivering her third child and again was given the gas. The man in white was there telling her the same things as before, but there were fewer forms approaching. The same experience occurred when her fourth and fifth child were born. During the latter, she told the man she now understood there would be more bodies for spirits. He agreed saying each one was a spirit coming to her. I was reminded of the personal nature of NDEs when she said she felt no need to tell others of her experience. Her husband did not want so many children and was upset each time she got pregnant. She, on the other hand, felt sure the Lord wanted her to have them and would make sure she did, regardless of the contraceptives she used to prevent them. Her sixth child came as a surprise and they planned to tie her tubes right after delivery. At the time of birth she again conversed with the man in white. She saw two remaining forms, one of which was very close. They moved closer with the roaring sound. At delivery, she noted to the man in white that there was one more form. He agreed, saying there would be another body for that one. She found it strange when her doctor came in after the birth stating she was too swollen to have her tubes tied. Although he intended for it to be done after six weeks, she never returned. Instead, she had an IUD inserted two years later. Four years passed and she was shocked to find herself pregnant again. She planned to definitely have her tubes tied following this delivery. Again, the man in white was at the birth. There had been only one form coming, and there were no more in the distance. He said that was all of them and there wouldn't be any more. Three hours later her tubes were tied. She had no regrets because the man in white had shown her that she had accepted all the spirits intended for her. I could not help being intrigued by such accounts.

Like the NDE, interesting information regarding the spirit and future events is imparted to the experiencers. PBEs also have features in common such as celestial light, beings radiating love, statements regarding when they're to come to a family and having a specific mission, as well as other things. They may deliver a message regarding something the parents need to do, impart a warning, or even provide a type of guardian protection.

It was especially interesting to read of a child in spirit contacting a future father, grandparent, or aunt. Sometimes they strongly appealed to more than one member of the family in their desire to be born. Some families did not wish to have another child and did so solely because of a PBE.

To me, what's most remarkable is how often the children eventually born turn out to look exactly as they appeared in the dream or vision, with the correct gender and physical characteristics, such as red curly hair. Sometimes the preborn spirit appears to the parent in

...ventually grows up to be that very

...ture are not limited to this book
...es during hypnotherapy. For ex-
...pected psychiatrist was practicing
...on a patient. As described in *Life
Between Life*, co......red by Joel L. Whitton, M.D., Ph.D.,
and Joe Fisher, Dr. Whitton's worded command that the
patient go back to a life before she was "Martha" led to a
strange response. She said she was in the sky, above a
farmhouse in the early morning. When asked what she
was doing up in the air, she answered, "I'm . . . waiting to
. . . be . . . born." She went on to say she was watching her
mother who was having difficulty filling a bucket. Her
baby body was weighing her mother down, and she
wanted to tell her to take care for both their sakes. Again,
the idea of a spirit's awareness before entering the
mother's womb is put forward. In another of Dr. Whitton's
subjects, a woman tells of being in the delivery room
watching her mother surrounded by medical personnel.
She herself is part of some white light and, as such, is
reluctant to merge with the new infant body and enter
this life. Dr. Whitton's patients knew why they were coming to earth and were involved in the planning. There's a
need to learn lessons and honor karmic unfoldment.
Karma is that balance sheet of eventually reaping exactly
what you've sown, or "what goes around, comes around."
The authors stress that we are the ones who do the
choosing of our future parents and lives and are thus responsible for who we are and the circumstances we
find ourselves in. In the chapter on karma entitled "The
Cosmic Classroom," the authors conclude with the following:

"The most important conclusion to be drawn from the
idea of karma is that chance has played no part in ar-
ranging the circumstances in which we find ourselves.

On Earth, we are the personification of choices that have been made in the bardo [between-life existence]. Our discarnate decision making has assigned us to our situation in life and, through subconscious inclination, continues to bring forth the bouquets and brickbats of destiny."

I quote these comments here because when all is said and done, I believe this is how it works. The main events of a life such as birth, death, and tragedies are scripted. I don't mean the universe is a giant wishing well which we run. It's God's design. It's His rules. Karma is His version of justice, and as we operate within His system, ultimately it's His will that is done. I realize some cannot conceive of God having a role in negativity, but their limits on what God shouldn't tolerate does not limit Him in reality. This is just my opinion, however, and I am far from the possessor of absolute truth. Unlike others, I do not equate my opinions or conclusions with absolute truth. After all, we can always be wrong.

Nevertheless, Dr. Whitton's conclusions are similar to those made by Brian Weiss, M.D., in his best-selling book, *Many Lives, Many Masters.* I recommend this fascinating account of Dr. Weiss's experiences with past-life regression therapy. Dr. Michael Newton, a hypnotherapist, goes further in his book, *Journey of Souls,* telling how regressed patients described choosing their future lives after somehow being able to view more than one! Some were pressured into choosing certain lives because of other karmically related souls who already planned to be there as relatives or because lessons to be learned by someone in that situation were just what the individual needed. If this is really the case, it's like the earth drama is already planned and we souls are the theater troupe deciding which parts we're going to take. I know that won't sound entirely strange to fans of the Bible Code, who believe the unfolding story of humanity has been encoded in the ancient document, including all of our names and birth dates!

Prebirth awareness has also been put forward by eminent psychiatrist Ian Stevenson, M.D., in his research of cases suggestive of reincarnation, as well as by Carol Bowman in her book *Children's Past Lives*. Edgar Cayce's data suggested that the soul enters the body shortly before birth, shortly after, or at the moment of birth. He went much further in his assessment of prenatal awareness as his readings gave details on subjects' past incarnations. Although resisting the notion of reincarnation due to his faith, he eventually accepted what was continually coming across in his readings. He knew about his own past lives and even revealed once in a reading that he would return in a future life in Nebraska in 2100. The spiritual enlightenment he received from the readings may have changed some previously held religious beliefs regarding reincarnation, but it, remarkably, did not change his view of an omnipotent, yet personal God. Despite this, he believed that man had free will and must take responsibility for his actions. Thus, it may be true that predetermination involves the scripted events—the cards you're dealt and may even have chosen—and free will is the way you play them.

Before you decide it's all too much to believe, consider the tale of the twins. Two males sharing space in their mother's womb argue over what their future holds. One insists that when their time is done, they will begin a completely different life. They will no longer exist in a fluid environment, but an air-filled one in which they'll breathe. They'll no longer be bent over. Instead, their bodies will straighten to eventually walk on their feet. They'll engage in activity in a new world that is currently inconceivable to them. His brother thinks this is all ridiculous. He states there is nothing beyond their womb existence. It's sort of like I used to think of life after death.

I couldn't imagine anything else beyond my present existence. Could I really enter a new world in a different form? No way. Well, the story ends when the first brother is about to be born. He is mourned by his twin who believes he will be gone forever, a fear confirmed by the scream of his brother after the delivery. He faces his own birth with abject fear, thinking it will be his end. We know that he will be pleasantly surprised to find out how wrong he was. If you identify more with the closed-minded twin, you might reconsider your views on life after death or life before life. Of course, if you're open-minded with regard to PBEs, you might wonder if such a conversation could actually have occurred!

In any event, this fascinating concept of preborn beings with planned missions and lessons dovetails well with the near-death experience. It appears mortal life may indeed be a brief sojourn on earth away from our true home, heaven, or a spiritual realm.

So what are we supposed to be doing here, again?

8

————⟨◆⟩————

The Illusory Nature of Time

The near-death and prebirth experiences seem to reveal one reason we're here: soul growth. The first time I heard of this concept, it was nearly incomprehensible to me. It was when I read *We Don't Die,* the book about George Anderson.

In one of George's most remarkable communications, the spirit of a teenage boy convinces his family that he indeed lives on and still cares about them. Although the specific information imparted to them was amazing, I was dumbstruck at the boy's response to his mother's question of why he died so young. George relayed, "Soul growth for you, your husband; your family, himself . . . It's a lesson to be learned by everybody, including himself." I had to stop reading at this point because these words made no sense to me. I guess I didn't really believe in the human soul. It was hard enough to imagine some nebulous distillate of my present self existing after death, let alone its having an agenda. Despite this, many a near-death experiencer has reported his consciousness leaving at the moment of bodily death only to be told at some point to return to complete what he came to do. So it seems the soul or spirit is the inner you who at least initially transits unchanged.

It's not all that far-fetched for me personally because, in retrospect, the improved person I became could not have been achieved with a lesser experience. My husband surprised me recently with the admission that this was true for him as well. What's so important about improving as a person or soul compared with the enormity of a tragedy? Like it or not, this soul growth may well be what life is about. Still, it's irresistible to think: If God really existed and was in control, He wouldn't allow terrible things to occur. He wouldn't want us to suffer. We may be bad, but we're not *that* bad. Sometimes, all we can see is the devastation staring us in the face. But if the truth lies in the lofty concepts thus far discussed, we need to know about it and incorporate it into our approach to life. To put it all in proper perspective, we need to look at the illusory nature of time. I'm not going to make any profound statements about time or discuss the theory of relativity. I'm simply going to ask that you withdraw from your stance between the trees, step back, and look at the overall forest.

Not long ago, a friend with terminal cancer told me that she could not see how God could want this for her or her family, or how any good could come of it. I mentioned that she was only looking at it from the perspective of this life. If she was convinced that her soul or spirit survived death, and even existed before she was born, she'd see this experience in a new context. It would be, as Edgar Cayce believed, a short foray in the ongoing life of her soul or a learning experience of relatively short duration. She would not entertain this possibility. To me, this self-imposed limitation is illogical. If one doesn't allow oneself to take a serious look at others' ideas, he or she can't legitimately accept or reject them. A minimal degree of open-minded thinking is necessary for one to learn of any truth that may not be to his liking. We can't only deal with what we like. We must deal with the truth as best we can determine it. In order to discover what that is, we have to look at all sides of an issue with reasonable fairness. Yet, this reluctance to consider opposing views is all too common. It is seen in simple, narrow-minded people as well as great scientists. Twenty years before he fancied himself a "tamed metaphysicist," Einstein stated that he could not, nor would he *want to*, conceive of an individual that survives his own physical death.

Rabbi Harold Kushner wrote in his book, *When Bad Things Happen to Good People*, "I am offended by those who suggest that God creates retarded children so that those around them will learn compassion and gratitude." Since when do we judge the merit of an idea by whether it appeals to us emotionally? He's offended so we should throw the possible truth out the window? I think a consideration of time's illusory nature will help here.

Consider the fact that a time period seems longer or shorter depending on what experiences fill it. As a seven-year-old child, I thought I'd have to wait forever to grow up. By the time I was seventeen, I had reached adult height and proportions, was driving myself to college, and no longer had any interest in hurrying time. The "forever" to grow up was actually ten years. Contrast those with the ten years from age twenty to thirty which seemed to fly by. Or simply consider the fact that a half-hour waiting for a friend to show up can be insufferable or no big deal if you happen to bring along interesting reading material. The way we experience time varies with one's frame of reference. Perhaps the seventy-five-year life span we have on earth is as short in relation to the life of a soul as a single night's dream is to an entire mortal lifetime. Ironically, one near-death experiencer said that upon first leaving the physical body, he felt more awake and became "the real me." This sounds sort of like waking from a dream. You're now really up and aware of who you are and what your situation is.

A famous rabbi once thought tragedies were supposed to happen to selfish, dishonest people. It was his job to comfort such individuals by assuring them of God's love. Luckily, they were unaware that he secretly thought they deserved their fate. His thinking radically changed when he later suffered a terrible tragedy himself. It would seem, according to his theory, that meant he was really despicable deep down. Unthinkable. He knew that *he* had been a good person; thus, his previous suppositions had to be false. Does this mean members of his congregation would now benefit from his new insight? No, because he decided that while God may have created the world, He had no hand in causing or preventing bad outcomes. Powerless, He could only cry with us. This weakened version of God was described in the rabbi's best-selling book and many readers who suffered tragedies accepted it. He was, after all, supposed to be something of an expert in these matters. He strongly rejected the view of another rabbi who believed suffering came to ennoble man, purge his thoughts of pride and superficiality, to expand his horizons, and in sum, repair that which is faulty in the personality. It's funny that he disagreed with this notion because that's exactly what does happen. This disagreement highlighted the conflict between his stated belief in the human soul and a seeming inability to consider anything beyond this life.

Prior to his tragedy, this rabbi-turned-author believed in an omnipotent God. I couldn't help imagining what his thinking would be if, instead of experiencing the real life tragedy, it took place inside of a nightmare. While dreaming, the events would appear to really be happening. He would know of no other reality. He would feel awful, wishing it wasn't true, but with no apparent escape. Upon awakening, he'd say something like, "Thank God that was just a dream. This is real life and no one's died." If someone were to then ask if he still believed in an omnipotent God, he'd probably say yes. He might say that although it was bad while it was happening, it's only one bad night out of his life and certainly won't change his ideas about an all-powerful God.

Yet, his real life experience may be like one difficult night in the life of his soul. If near-death experiences tell us anything, it's that a spiritual realm exists, and it's there that the soul or spirit operates out of. Tolstoy wrote, "Our life is but one of the dreams of that more real life, and so it is endless until the last one, the very real life, the life of God." So, we're in good company here.

Ironically, the rabbi has since become much more compassionate as a result of his devastation. This would support the "learning experience" theory despite his views. He no longer looks at those in tragic circumstances as selfish, dishonest people who deserve what they get. I'm sure he identifies with and comforts them to a much greater degree than he previously had. Yet, instead of thinking an all-powerful God intended his suffering to ennoble him, purge his thoughts of pride, and repair that which was faulty in his personality, he can't see the forest through the trees.

It's hard to open one's mind because altering established views of reality is destabilizing. Without consciously thinking about it, people strenuously avoid doing this. I remember when I told one of my sisters about my enhanced belief in God and spiritual existence. She adamantly resisted the latter subject. This loving family member, who ordinarily would have indulged any fanciful take I had on our tragedy to aid a grief-stricken sister, instead clashed openly with me. Imagine a bereaved mother debating that her son does *so* go on. My sister's belief system at that moment was more important to her than my grief. People desperately hold onto their view of reality without realizing how important it is to them.

In any event, it is my belief that tragedies are momentary hurts necessary for our greater good. It's like a child's vaccination. The loving mother leads the child into the doctor's office. The child trusts this woman who has always cared for him and prevented him from harm. Everything is going well and suddenly there's intense pain where an injection has just been administered. He cries, experiencing only the pain of the moment and thinking, "How could my mother, the ruler of my world, let this happen to me?" The truth is that she sought out this painful treatment because it was a momentary discomfort for his greater good. Like the child, we sufferers of tragedy are in the middle of the painful moment. We thought our Father loved us, yet He let this happen. Ultimately, we will understand how it's for our greater good. But for now, we're in the middle of the scream. As Buddha said, "A lifetime is a mere flash of lightning in the scheme of things." I continually strive to see past the illusory nature of time. I now realize my years of intense suffering were the prolonged "moment" I had to weather to emerge as a better human being.

9

—— ⟨◆⟩ ——

It Should Make Sense

I remember being told years ago that one was not allowed to study the mystical teachings of Judaism known as Kabbalah until reaching age forty. I assumed this was because a certain level of maturity was needed. After all, this body of knowledge included information on the nature of God, reincarnation, and a measure-for-measure type of karma. Today, I think the age restriction had more to do with one's being at a point in life when what I call his "program" had already kicked in. The program is the major life trial one suffers through that profoundly changes him. It can change who he thinks he is or, for the spiritually minded, the quality of his soul. This could be a great tragedy, struggle, or series of lesser problems that cause one to wonder about the meaning of life and/or God.

Every life is a mixed bag of joys and sorrows. Barring any exceptions, this is true for anyone who lives to see the measure of his years. There is no such thing as a charmed life. If you think you know someone who's having a charmed life, then one of two things is true: You don't know their whole story or their main program has not kicked in.

I used to think that most of the celebrities' hardships featured in the tabloids were a result of life in the fast lane. I'm still aware of the challenges of fame, but I now see celebrities as a group who can neither maintain the secrecy of their tragedies nor share the details only at their discretion. There's no tragedy club for such individuals. Instead, all of their troubles are broadcast to us on a regular basis. If you read the tabloids long enough, you'll be assured that everyone has a program. It may take twenty or thirty years to kick in, but inevitably it will.

In the case of a child's death, the child may be providing the program for the parents. What benefit do the children reap? For that matter, what about people who have suffered tortured or extremely impoverished lives? The metaphysical value of these may seem obscure, but it would be incomprehensible in the absence of an afterlife. Knowledge of an afterlife means their suffering is temporary and upon death, they will be welcomed into a loving environment. Although some traumas experienced for the soul's learning involve concepts beyond understanding from our present perspective, there is one thing I know for certain. The notion that God created humankind and the world and then lost control of His creation is absurd. He is always in control. Some people are uncomfortable with this idea because they think it suggests punishment or an unfavorable judgment during difficult times. More often, it's an aversion to predetermination. Less free will means less personal power. This is disturbing because it's essentially a loss of control. Who wants to be walking through a script even if it's God's? They view themselves as existentialists, not fatalists. Maybe Forrest Gump was right in thinking it's actually a little of both. Although humans are supposed to have free will, there is disagreement on just what level we have it. Some say we only have it while we're on earth which is how we incur bad karma. In other words, we're responsible for what we do here because we continually choose our actions. Others say we are behaving in a less spontaneous manner as we respond to our subconscious dictates, which are serving up the program our soul planned with *its* free will. Even if you subscribe to the former idea, it's clear we don't have complete free will on earth. No one *chooses* to lose their mother from a terminal illness, nor are they able to prevent the death because they choose to. So, while some things are clearly out of our hands, our concern with free will lies in the way we handle the curve balls, what attitudes we adopt toward the many aspects of life, and how we conduct ourselves in general. What counts is what we take away from our experiences, or what we learn.

The numerous examples of future events being seen or prophesied suggests the story of mankind may already be written or, at least, it's somehow out there and able to be tapped. If each individual is unique and behaves according to the inclinations of his personality, doesn't that defy accurate prediction? I believe the Creator is so awesome that He anticipates all of our actions in advance and thus knows the future. He possibly wrote the story Himself. C.S. Lewis, the famed author, once wrote that history is a story written by the finger of God. Personally, I firmly believe that the main elements of our lives are scripted, divine in origin, and therefore, meant to be. These would include birth, death, genius ability, great beauty, and disfigurement. Even such things as amputations, paralysis, or terminal illness may be a part of one's program. Each provides its own lessons. We just may not be seeing the difference between a prewritten story and spontaneous free will. And if we can't detect any encroachment on our will, does it really matter?

If I am correct about the meant-to-be-ness of events, you couldn't help wonder why God would want a buffoon to be a world leader or about the reasons for a host of other things that seem to make no sense. This is, after all, the One who created darkness and light and everything from nothing. His purposes may be beyond us, but they are sure. In fact, if there truly is such a thing as reincarnation, its purpose is probably to let one see life in someone else's shoes or from all different vantage points. Experiencing various trials firsthand would certainly make one more compassionate, wise, and tolerant.

Of course, much of this is speculation. Yet, it makes more sense than some age-old mainstream views which fly in the face of logic. Let's have fun with some of these, shall we?

Dead is dead. That's our natural end. People generally fear death. Why do we recoil at the inevitable obliteration of our consciousness if it's natural? The answer is that deep down we know we're not supposed to end, thus the thought is very disturbing. Like many others, my eighty-six-year-old grandmother insisted she was "not ready" just days before she succumbed to congestive heart failure. When such individuals have predeath visitations from deceased family members to aid their passing, they stop fearing death. They become aware of continuing on elsewhere with loved ones and not ceasing to exist.

We come into this world alone, and we go out alone. What a depressing thought. Those who have had predeath visitations and near-death experiences insist we don't go out alone. I bet we don't come in alone either. In fact, a number of regression therapists have reported hearing patients' earliest memories under hypnosis in which they described being escorted to their mother's womb.

We're just smart animals who were unlucky enough to become aware of our own mortality. When I was a small child, my sister told me something like this. I couldn't believe it. She pointed out the anatomic features we had that were similar to those of animals. I understood, but insisted I was more like a computer. I thought I was special and somehow better than the animals. Evolution teaches us that we're just some primates' descendants. My original ideas were closer to the truth. We are divine sparks. We are children of God or, if you prefer, tiny consciousness subsets of Universal Consciousness. Although clothed in bodies of flesh like animals, we are capable of building a sophisticated society. If there was ever a group placed on earth to cocreate with God, it's us. This concrete distinction from other animals speaks for itself, but it's amazing how godless individuals trivialize it. Bereaved parents are acutely aware of this. Unlike animals, the parents often dwell solely on their loss, not their other children. Animals are supposed to be concerned with the survival of the species, thus one would think they'd quickly concentrate on their surviving young. The broken bond between a human mother and her deceased child appears to be on a soul level, often rendering her uncaring of whether she lives or dies as well as her ongoing mothering role. So much for survival of the species. Fortunately, providence often steps in, aiding the situation, until enough healing occurs for parents to be operational again.

It's ridiculous the way people throughout history have concerned themselves with a Supreme Being whether it be tribal worship, cults, or organized religion. What a waste of energy! We have this need precisely because we're not just animals negotiating our survival. We're part spirit. We are, in fact, spiritual beings with spiritual needs. We hunger for love all through our lives, not just during a mating season. We seek a divine connection. If religion or love relationships don't satisfy these needs, we fill the emptiness with drugs, food, material things, new relationships, cults, new age gurus, or any of a host of other substitutes.

Why do our mothers often fail to love us unconditionally? We deserve it, and hopefully we'll find it in a mate if we didn't get it growing up. We believe we're entitled to this because we come from a heavenly place of unconditional love. We loved getting it and life often seems cold without it. This is why our mothers are subject to such abundant criticism and often come up wanting. After receiving God's unconditional love, we arrive here holding this poor mortal woman responsible for the continuation of such a love. After all, a mother is the closest thing on earth to a provider of selfless love.

There's no absolute truth or justice. These are easily distorted and often in the eye of the beholder. There are so many ways of looking at a situation and rationalizing negative behavior that it seems we're always in a gray area. There are such things as absolute truth and justice and that's why they're important to us. We know on some level that we're all ultimately accountable for our actions. If more skeptics consciously believed this to be true, that God saw to it, then they would behave in a more admirable fashion. If everyone knew that they, themselves, would experience what they'd done to others, as near-death experiencers who have undergone a life review assert, the world would be a much different place.

The first time you beat incredible odds is when you win life's lottery of eggs and sperm, resulting in your birth. After all, your mother had countless eggs in her ovaries, of which few are released over a reproductive lifetime, and your father released several million sperm with each ejaculate, multiplied by all the times he'd done so. You're so lucky to be here. Not really. You're not a one-in-a-billion winner. You, the spirit, were coming to earth to do the "earth thing" and fulfill your mission. If a different egg and sperm resulted in conception, then the physical vehicle you enliven would be a little different. In any event, you were coming, no matter what.

It's important to avoid life's pitfalls. They interfere with your plans. This is not exactly paradise and we re not here to have a trouble-free life with a guarantee of happiness. This life is *about learning,* especially by overcoming adversity and handling obstacles. In some ways, the long, uneventful, harmonious periods aren't the norm but the recovery or resting periods between challenges. I personally try not to get too comfortable. "Constant careful happiness" is good advice.

Life has no real purpose. Of course, it does. I always wondered why people who think this way aren't more hedonistic. Clearly, the goal is not to live as long as possible and die with the most toys. Life is like a proving ground or summer camp. You enjoy and learn from experience, but when it gets too challenging and devoid of love, you despair and want to go home. You get to go home only when you've completed the program. When a child dies, it's like they get to go home early. The trial is the parents'. Even when they know the child's spirit continues on, the endless separation is what is so painful. I regret not being able to do the "earth thing" with Roy.

There have been so many reports of ghost sightings, apparitions, angels, mystical visions, and miracles. It's hard to believe that all the experiencers are liars or have overactive imaginations. It's a lot of smoke for no fire. Correct. The true experiences are all part of the leaks between the spiritual and physical worlds. We have to be subtly aware of our divinity, but not to the point where we're not concerned with our roles in the material world. This life must be taken seriously for us to learn the lessons we came here for. Thus, knowledge of God is, for most, a question of faith, not certainty. Despite the reassurance that the belief in my divinity offers, I never lose sight of my place here. I was born into a family, a religion, and a region, all of which is no accident. Since there's no way to be certain of these lofty concepts or even my purpose, I simply live my life in the role I find myself. I don't rely on guardian spirits. I mean, the idea of a divine presence is comforting because I can't control everything in life, but I don't dwell on it. Spirituality simply strengthens me so I can do the "earth thing" despite our tragedy. I care for my children, work, pursue my interests, revere God in my own way, and try to enjoy life. In other words, I can't get lost in the spiritual aspect of life because I have a job to do here. Spiritual escape is not an option. After all, if you don't engage your program, why be here?

I just think it should make sense.

10

❮◆❯

Now What?

Whatever else can be said about time, it does heal. Even after a tragedy, a healing will occur with the passing of months and years. This healing is not like the one following an illness or minor injury. You're never "good as new" again. Yet, in a lot of ways, you're probably better. In the case of a child's death, the loss becomes part of the parent like an amputee's loss is now part of him. He no longer awakens with the first thought "My leg is gone!" but he is acutely aware of it as he maneuvers out of bed. In the beginning, I used to wake up with the first thought being "Oh no, Roy's dead." These days I wake up equally aware of my situation, but I instead think, "Oh yeah, the new life again."

In spite of this, grieving parents often become more relaxed and at peace than others. Aside from no longer

69

having to fear the worst because it's already happened, this newfound peace may be due to a rearranging of their priorities or the fact they no longer feel held to previous standards. Their soul searching and reflection frequently brings a new understanding and, thus, a different perspective.

My search for meaning brought discoveries about life which enhanced my existence. I felt deeper, more knowledgeable, insightful, and in tune. Unfortunately, I stepped out into the world and found it had not changed. The same, silly things were considered important. People exhibited their same irritating ways and boastfulness, but I was less tolerant.

What to do? I'd like to humbly offer some advice to those who have recently suffered a tragedy. We don't live in a vacuum, although sometimes it's tempting to structure your life as though you do. First, be mindful that others don't realize this loss continues to be a big part of your life. While you don't want to discuss it, you may feel you must or they'll dominate the conversation with their irritating content. In short, avoid severely draining people. If you can't, there's a useful book called *Mental Shielding* by Richard Driscoll. It's more like a booklet accompanied by a cassette tape that teaches you to create a mental shield against hostility among other things. The technique can be learned in a couple of days and can be invaluable for some. Difficulties in dealing with others will improve over time, in any case. Just looking at others in a new way can help. For example, their bragging simply shows their insecurities and what they consider important. Understand what you're seeing and be glad you're past it. It's not always easy. I don't know how many times someone went on and on about their kid not getting into the right school or not being popular, and I wanted to shake them and say, "Your kid's alive. Try to remember what's really important."

Others may have expectations which represent their idea of what you should be doing and maybe what you used to be concerned with. A simple pat answer such as, "This death has me rethinking how things will go" is sufficient. Be aware that you may occasionally be caught off guard by a very insensitive comment. If you've suffered a genuine tragedy, you won't just get insulted, you'll *reel*. Just knowing in advance this happens may help. It may surprise you when others don't honor your spiritual notions. They may come out and say, "Whatever gets you through it or helps you cope" or "Whatever you believe," as though you're some feeble fool who has to lie to themselves. To me, these people are selfish and destructive because they put their need to assert their own beliefs over any concern about offending you. You may encounter those who disagree if you say it might have been meant to be, thus, in some cases, implying it was your fault and you're trying to deny it! They could have kept such thoughts to themselves. Instead, they chose to rub salt in a wound in the name of honesty. Yet, are they scrupulously honest in all other areas of their lives? Invariably, not. Please trust me when I say these are very wrongheaded, judgmental individuals whose flaws, in time, Providence will correct. I know it corrected mine.

All of this is not to suggest you will be overwhelmed by insensitive clods. Most people we dealt with were incredibly compassionate. In fact, the entire community embraced us in a way we hadn't expected. It helped renew us and taught us compassion by example. So, why have I focused so much on the negativity you can absorb from other people? Inadvertently, the result can be a severely depressed mood.

After reeling from a tragic blow, you soon find yourself on an emotional roller coaster. This may sound surprising, because you'd think there would be only downs and no ups. In fact, a labile state of mood swings ensues that leaves you continually trying to regain control. The cause of the depression, the tragic event, cannot be changed. Family and/or spiritual support are essential and a grief counselor or bereavement group like the Compassionate Friends may be extremely helpful.

The problem of mood swings is a tricky moment-to-moment thing. One moment, you're okay. The next, you're miserable because a well-meaning friend made a sympathy call mandating the discussion of upsetting memories from which you had taken a mental reprieve. One moment, you're immersed in the activities of daily living, thinking you just might make it. The next, you're suicidal because you saw or read something that triggered intensely painful emotions. Talking with an understanding friend or family member helps diffuse these as does writing in a journal.

Writing is very beneficial. Simply putting your feelings on paper is therapeutic, even if you're not "that type." If you have a good or bad experience with others, write about it in a notebook or even on scraps of paper. It may also stimulate that inner voice with advice or caring words for yourself. Write that, too. If that would never happen, then imagine what you've written is a friend's experience. Write what you would honestly say to comfort them or the reason you would cut them slack. Why shouldn't those kind words apply to you? It's amazing how helpful our own advice is. Not only does writing about emotions decrease their momentary power, but it is all very healing on the reread. If you're grieving, writing about a meaningful coincidence or unusual event that appears to suggest a spiritual origin means you can't easily dismiss it later as the memory fades. For example, if you see or sense the spirit of a deceased loved one, the written account not only prevents you from talking yourself out of it, but serves as a continuing source of com-

BUSINESS REPLY MAIL

FIRST CLASS   PERMIT NO. 2456   VIRGINIA BEACH, VA

POSTAGE WILL BE PAID BY ADDRESSEE

**ASSOCIATION FOR RESEARCH
AND ENLIGHTENMENT INC
215 67TH STREET
VIRGINIA BEACH VA 23451-9819**

SEEKING INFORMATION ON

holistic health, spirituality, dreams, intuition or ancient civilizations?

Call 1-800-723-1112, visit our Web site, or mail in this postage-paid card for a FREE catalog of books and membership information.

Name: _____

Address: _____

City: _____

State/Province: _____

Postal/Zip Code: _____ Country: _____

Association for Research and Enlightenment, Inc.
215 67th Street
Virginia Beach, VA 23451-2061

For faster service, call 1-800-723-1112.
www.edgarcayce.org

PBIN

fort. Some bereaved parents recall premonitory dreams about their child's death which they'll record after the tragedy to support a gut feeling that it was unavoidable. Intense dreams after a tragedy may actually include a genuine visit from the deceased, providing comfort when reread in a journal. Other dreams should be recorded as well because they offer insights into personal issues you may have difficulty facing. Once understood, these may be dealt with, as a repetitive theme can often be identified in a series of properly interpreted dreams. You can even tell how well you're handling it, and later, if there's an improvement. This is not as difficult as you think. Elements in dreams have symbolic meanings which can be looked up in a dream dictionary. Not just any dream dictionary will do. I like Tony Crisp's *Dream Dictionary* and Sandra Thompson's *Cloud Nine*. Even though several meanings may be given for a particular dream symbol, somehow you know which applies to you. It may not even be a standard meaning but only your symbol for something, and yet, you'll know that after a while, too. I kept having dreams with a faltering self-confidence theme. I rejected this because confidence is not and never has been my problem. Who cares about that, anyway, when you're suffering a tragedy? Despite this, I went on to have dreams where my face was scarred from acid. When I looked up "face," "scar," and "acid" as well as other things, it was obvious that the intensely emotional experience I suffered left a residue that bothered me greatly on some level and hurt my confidence or the face I show others. And I thought I didn't care at all what others thought! Thus, knowing where you truly are emotionally is important. Your dream interpretations may not always be correct, but recording them in a journal often reveals an undeniable pattern. I can just hear some psychologist telling me I interpreted my dreams wrong. It's *my* experience, doctor, remember? Besides, knowing your interpretations can be wrong means you don't have to take them to heart. There's a good chance you've identified important concerns, but you're never 100 percent sure, so you needn't obsess over it.

What else can you do to keep your mood even? Ideally, the best antidepressant I can recommend is aerobic exercise for at least thirty minutes, three or four times a week. Aside from releasing brain chemicals that result in mood elevation, there's an accompanying sense of accomplishment that makes exercise the biggest favor you can do yourself. Many times, how you look at life has more to do with your mood than what's going on. I used to exercise with tears in my eyes, or all-out crying, sure that I was effecting a mood change. When I was done, my sadness would lift. It's not about your appearance or even health. It's *therapy*. The problem is, understandably, devastated individuals often refuse to perform exercise of any kind. If that's true for you, keep it in the back of your mind that exercise should eventually become part of your lifestyle. Exercise is key in treating and preventing recurrent depression.

What should be done in the meantime? There are those who say we are too quick to anesthetize psychological pain in the modern world. I believe grieving parents should be exempted from such judgment. This places me at odds with some prominent individuals. World famous psychiatrist Elisabeth Kübler Ross, addressing grieving parents, once wrote, "Never allow anybody to give you Valium at the time of such a crisis as it will cheat you out of the choice to experience all your feelings, cry out all your pain, shed all your tears so that you can live again, not only for your own sake, but for the sake of your family and all others whose life you can touch." If this rings true for you, follow her advice. I'm not a psychiatrist, but I am a physician who had a child die tragically. No matter how tranquilized, you cannot avoid any aspect of the experience. *Life doesn't let you.* From the beginning, you're trying to keep some kind of grip as best you can. The pain is so raw and intense, I'm amazed there are people that *don't* take something. This doesn't mean I recommend being so numb that you don't experience much of anything. I would, however, recommend the new selective serotonin reuptake inhibitor, or SSRI, antidepressants to grieving parents, particularly those having suicidal thoughts. Obtaining a prescription should not be difficult as many physicians are comfortable with these drugs. They appear safer than their older counterparts, requiring less monitoring and fewer daily doses. In fact, a current concern is they're being given "like water" for minor problems. Their action is said to be in allowing serotonin, the chemical messenger associated with well being, to remain in the areas between brain cells.

I like these drugs because they do not make one feel artificially happy, nor are they numbing. They appear to take the great edge off, so you can be well aware of your situation, but not overwhelmed by it. You are able to think clearly and perform duties, experiencing little or no side effects, in most cases. If one had the luxury of having no pressing responsibilities, such as other children to care for or gainful employment, it might make sense to take no medication, lay down, and cry for months. However, most of us are bound by our roles. We may need to keep jobs and behave appropriately while there. There are often other children to consider, as in my case. These children will also be suffering the loss, possibly experiencing survivor's guilt. The focus of the child's world is the caretaking parent. The parent sets the tone.

By behaving responsibly, parents assure that their children feel secure and loved. Although they saw my sadness, I was affectionate with my children and encouraged discussion. I tried to maintain as normal a home situation as I could. If a parent withers in a private world of grief, constantly crying over a child's death for months, the other children can be devastated. This commonly occurs, and can be perceived by the surviving siblings as parental favoritism for the dead child. This sad scenario may be avoided in cases where the parent takes a mild antidepressant. Certainly, it's not necessary in all cases, but it's something to consider. The medication is intended for only a limited time and is given under the watchful eye of the prescribing physician. When the bereaved feels stronger, the medicine may be tapered off. The emotional disconnect caused by the antidepressant will then cease. At that point, he sort of wakes up to his life and experiences sadness, but to a much lesser degree than in the acute period. Besides grieving parents, others in tragic circumstances may also benefit from SSRI-type antidepressants. One friend, dying of terminal cancer, found she could not enjoy life at all during her final year. She wanted to, and was mostly pain free, but the bleakness of the diagnosis prevented her. This changed after she started one of these drugs. She said the difference was like "night and day." Another cancer patient, a nurse, was not terminal, but the sadness caused by just having the disease, undergoing the treatment, and not knowing if she'd eventually die from it, drove her to distraction. She couldn't work because of this and was, thus, kept from what she enjoyed most. After starting a similar antidepressant, she was back at work, surprised that she could once again do what she loved.

Self-help books can be beneficial, but read them carefully. We tend to elevate the so-called experts to a level where their written words are taken as absolute truth. Sometimes, what they're preaching is just not right for you. In fact, it may not be right at all. If advice doesn't seem valuable to you, forget it. In one book on grieving, there was much emphasis on funeral preparation and visiting the gravesite. It seemed like they were saying to rub your nose in it, or it means you don't care enough or are not facing the reality as you should. I knew this advice would not only be wrong for me but destructive. As a spiritual woman, I know it's my child's body, like an outgrown overcoat that's buried. His spirit is around us often. If I want to honor him or express my love, I don't have to go where we laid the overcoat with a rock over it, and destroy myself. I can speak to him here at home just by calling out his name and summoning his spirit. You may be different. The gravesite may be a peaceful and welcoming place for you. What is important is that you do what feels right for you and only follow advice that's helpful.

Ultimately, you will choose whether or not you'll ever feel joy again. Some people feel guilty resuming their lives because it's like they're betraying the deceased in some way. I suspect my loved ones in spirit are doing a lot better than I am. You can only understand this if you believe in survival of the spirit. You'd know the people who loved you are still around and want you to be happy and at peace as they are. Although evidence of such survival is comforting, it doesn't automatically let you off the hook. It's a hook of your own making. You must release yourself, so that you may engage life again. Being able to eventually move on shows you've met the challenge and succeeded. Success in your program means the tragedy didn't happen in vain. You've fulfilled your purpose which is what the deceased and God wants for you. If you've been through this, you already know you've improved as a person in many ways. It actually crossed my mind once that if I didn't get past it and become better, it might mean I didn't learn the lesson and would require a similar one in the future. No thanks.

Lastly, I'd like to mention the survival strategies described here are especially important on anniversaries. These dates, such as the deceased's birthday, day of death, or day of tragedy, will sometimes sneak up on you. They may be extremely depressing so mentally bolster yourself beforehand. Arrange to be with loved ones or friends who are a comfort to you. Maybe plan on going away for a few days. This change of scenery might help more than you think. All in all, give it time and be kind to yourself. There honestly is a light at the end of the tunnel. Just take it one day at a time. Each day you get through is a day closer to successfully completing your time here.

11

---◆---

How Good Do We Have to Be?

Am I a good person? How good do I really have to be? This may sound surprising, but this question becomes a real issue for those who have reached the healing phase following a tragedy. With the exception of certain individuals who cannot move on, or simply lack insight into their own experiences, most feel there's a reason for their suffering and some kind of plan is in action. They may see it as God's or a universal plan in which they each have a role. How will they execute their roles? Some will just concentrate on making it through each day and not worry much about anyone else. Who could blame them after what they've been through? Interestingly, others try to be their best self, with the example of ideal human behavior taken from the Bible or other religious texts. The reason they bother is they've discovered, or perhaps always knew, that there is a God in control who created them and has some expectations.

I write this as though these are remarkable individuals with beliefs different from the rest of us. They shouldn't be all that different since recent polls cite over 90 percent of Americans claim to believe in God. But, do they really? There's clearly a humanist tendency in our mainstream thought which belies this assertion. The news media almost always assume a skeptical, if not godless, stance. Neuroscientists don't think a near-death experience can be anything other than a brain manifestation because, for most of them, there is no God or heaven. It is also seen in subtle ways like the extreme frustration when the justice system fails because there's no way God is going to make sure there's ultimate justice. There's no such thing, right? The abject fear of germs, cancer, unsafe car seats, infant sleeping positions, dangerously hard softballs, and inadequate bicycle helmets all tell of a people who think they must control every variable because there's nothing between them and a bad outcome. Certainly not God. This is not about putting safety first, and then trusting in God. He's really not a consideration. Things are all thought to be left up to chance. Thus, for much of that 90 percent, God is not involved, not caring, not real.

As I wrote in an earlier chapter, the unarticulated assumptions and age-old conflicted religious notions must be aired out to dispel the nonsensical God. For example, I never thought a punishing God made sense. He can't be small-minded. Upon airing that one out, I realized that His plan addresses our weaknesses. We each start out with these lacks, conceptually like a stick figure. The difficult lessons change us on a fundamental level, fleshing us out by adding depth, color, and understanding, among other things. He's not punishing us, but instead bringing us to the next level of learning. Without growth, one can't advance. It's like a child who can't advance to the third grade because he hasn't mastered second grade material. It doesn't matter how nice he is. Even if he was placed in the higher grade, he couldn't make sense of the new coursework and would go nowhere. We are continually evolving or getting fleshed out. A God who makes sense is often essential in acquiring true belief. It is my view that the lack of a genuine belief in God is responsible for much of our problems, both on the individual level, as well as for society as a whole. Only with this belief will we be able to figure out how good we have to be.

Without it, one can be as good as he likes. After all, there is no ultimate authority to answer to. No one is keeping track of our actions and assuring appropriate consequences. There is no objective set of rules to follow so we can make up our own as we go along, according to our liking.

If, on the other hand, one believes in his own divinity, that a Creator placed him here to have purposeful experiences, then he feels a responsibility to do the right thing. How good does God expect us to be? Reasonably, what standard should we hold ourselves to?

Some cite what the Bible says is expected of us. Others feel it's too difficult to comply with so they reject it entirely, or state it's just a book written by men, not God. For the most part, I subscribe to the biblical version of right and wrong. I think we need an objective standard for morality. We can't just arbitrarily decide what's right or wrong, because we will inevitably rationalize whatever behavior we wish to engage in or that others say is right for our times until we become clearly amoral.

However, I am far from the biblical version of the perfect person. I can simply do my best and continually try to be better. Holding myself to an impossible standard would be a set-up for constant failure. Preaching to others is also not my aim. I would just like us to agree on an objective code of behavior as revealed in the common thread of teachings of the world's major religions. We each could then aspire to be our best selves, and when we messed up, we'd admit it and not rewrite the rules.

As a bereaved parent, I don't relish putting heavy demands upon myself. So, here's my version for the minimal requirement of goodness. It's my philosophy of how to live according to Divine Will. I have two simple guides. First, there's the ten commandments. These are the basic "dos" (revere God, honor your parents) and "don'ts" (cheat, lie, steal) of life. For fine tuning, read those holy texts, because the rest, as they say, is commentary. The second guide, useful in just about all instances, is the advice that an unconditionally loving parent, who possessed a moral underpinning, would give you. This is consistent with Divine Will because that's exactly what God is to me. I mention the moral underpinning because an unconditionally loving parent may condone a crime committed by his child if he, himself, is not righteous.

That's it. I live according to those two guides and avoid the confusing opinions and attitudes that are constantly emerging in mainstream thought. If I'm tempted to do something wrong, I don't have to rationalize. The commandments are out there. If I break them in a situation with extenuating circumstances, I appeal to the unconditionally loving parent. Sometimes, I know the response would be that I was flat out wrong. Other times, it would be more like, "I understand what you did and it's all right." Through it all, I try to be a good person and see things from the other's point of view.

God has been described as judgmental, but more often loving and patient. He expects a lot from us, but ultimately, love seems to be most important to Him. He is willing to wait an eternity for sinners to repent. This is how we human parents may be described as well. We set down rules for our children and are dismayed when they break them. But, we always love them and hope that they'll eventually come around. It is this analogy that enables us to understand His love for us in a limited way and makes Him accessible as opposed to fearful.

I can just hear the complaints of those who would not view God as an unconditionally loving parent. I'm not just referring to agnostics and atheists. Those who deny God come in many forms, including spiritual. The brighter and more controlling the person, the more this may be true. A spiritual person who tries to reduce God to simply the life force behind the universe, refers to something one may strive to harness, control, or influence. They want to be in control of God, instead of the other way around! Then, there are those who paint Him as a great body of water and the rest of us are just like raindrops. This eliminates the parental type of caring, guidance, or control. It's pretty inert. Everyone's entitled to their own God concept, but many of these people have disdain for the parental sentiment as though it's a childish notion only the weak would adopt.

I have a theory as to why some people, particularly bright people, cannot stand the idea of a God in control or any parental attribute ascribed to Him. Aside from those who don't want to cede any of the credit for their accomplishments to the grace of God, they seem to transfer the type of relationship they had with their own parents, especially fathers, to their God concept. So, if one had a warm relationship with her mother, she'd welcome a God with maternal attributes. If one was treated poorly by his father, he may be uncomfortable with the Father-God concept. If he was raised to disdain childishness, he will reject the notion of being a sinning child subject to the judgment of an all powerful Parent. The parent-child relationship is seen as naive, more appropriate for an earlier era. It need not be viewed that way because it doesn't automatically mean God is a grandfatherly figure sitting on a throne. He is as inconceivable as ever, but the striking analogy elucidates his relationship to us. A Creator who is fulfilled through birthing of a sort, and allows his creations to be similarly fulfilled, makes it powerfully clear. He views us as we view our children. Contrast this with the modern idea that we are really God, but haven't realized it. This is not our reality and won't be until we reach a type of God-consciousness. After all, we are not fully in control on earth, and even when we die, our lives are reviewed in a process that doesn't appear to be of our making. Our final destination seems appropriate to what we've earned, as well as the quality of our consciousness, but its not where we actively chose to go. It sounds like Someone else is in control at the spiritual level. Thus, this we-are-God notion seems dishonest or, at least, not relevant to our current experience.

In any event, a genuine belief in God not only provides the proper context to how good we have to be, but makes our approach to life universally better. Every experience, good or bad, is meaningful. There's a reason it has occurred and is part of God's plan. Every living thing is related to every other. While we humans have dominion over the animals, we wouldn't abuse it as we'd respect God's creation and the trust He placed in us when he enlivened us with His divinity. We would look at our fellow man with true equality because we'd know that God made each of His children special and had no favorites. We are siblings in this sense. Skin color and religion are situational aspects that don't make us different on the inside, the divine part. It's there that we're very similar. We'd help each other out because that's what our Father would expect of His children, not because we were pushed or shamed into it. Certain debates would no longer be necessary if we all agreed that God puts each life in motion, and only He determines when it's finished. Thus, we wouldn't take lives, nor artificially prop them up at the very end. Our families, successes, possessions, lovers, and occupations wouldn't truly define us because our value would come from the inner spirit and its vast potential. There would be no need to obsess over what everyone else thought because it was thoroughly understood that no one was better than anyone else, nor worse. We would treat our neighbors the way we wished to be treated because we'd be sure to eventually "meet self," the definition of karma according to Edgar Cayce. Absolute justice would always be assured because there was a Witness to all of our actions who saw to it. Just being part of the grand design would make one want to do better. After putting forth one's best effort, one would leave the rest up to God and not sweat the small stuff. Can you imagine what the world would be like if everyone truly believed and trusted in God?

12

❬◆❭

Final Thoughts and Reflections

It's been some time since I wrote those words and their truth becomes more obvious to me with each passing day. I remain anchored to the Jewish faith and, in fact, have become more observant though still not a contender. Despite this, it's a secret thrill to be present at services knowing I have a greater certainty of God than most people in the room, including those leading the service. And unlike some of the others, I have a true respect for all of the world's monotheistic religions because I'm aware of their equally valid connection to God.

For me, God is not just "everywhere" or "love." He's a personal being who communicates things through meaningful coincidences. Recently, when I was at services, I listened while another congregant was thanked by the president of the temple. She had contributed the necessary funding for a sacred object newly obtained by the synagogue. I regretted that I wasn't the one who made the donation, because I had considered it but hadn't followed through. I felt that it was probably better this way because the contributor was one of those real contenders, a more ritualistic and observant Jew. A short time later, I happened to become aware that this same woman was giving an awful time to an honest man who had performed a service for her and expected payment. It wasn't the first time she behaved this way, either. She didn't want to pay this relatively small sum, yet, she'd given the temple a huge amount of money for which she was credited and publicly thanked numerous times. In an extremely unlikely turn of events, I happened to be in the right place at the right time to become aware of the truth of her shameful private behavior. I thought it was meant to be. God was showing me that those who sat in front in the temple were no more deserving, righteous, or closer to Him than I was.

Another time, we were invited to a holiday event at a church that my husband thought would be great fun for the children. Although people of all religions were invited, I had a feeling I might encounter some enthusiastic Christians eager to convince me that their way was best, to save me. I think that's fine for those in need of a connection to God, but me? I was a little reluctant, but we went anyway. On the way, I heard a song on the radio that I hadn't heard in years, "The Church of the Poisoned Mind" by Culture Club. Sure enough, I was met by people who did not respect my religion and wanted to bring me into theirs. The song helped because I felt it was God's way of giving me a head's up. He wasn't saying their beliefs were poisoned or poisonous. He was simply saying that even in the attempt to help people by ministering, the human filter to God's teaching can result in their acting in an ungodly way.

He's more obvious other times. I once ordered beautiful Egyptian handmade candlesticks which I planned to use for the Sabbath candle lighting. I started to have second thoughts about using them for this purpose because, well, we were slaves in Egypt and this was a sacred candle lighting. Anyway, a postal service delivered them on a Friday night at sundown, which is the time weekly when the candles are supposed to be lit, and I thought "He's telling me, 'Of course it's O.K. to use them.'"

I continue to be comforted by God's undeniable hand in the similarity of our sons because as my youngest grew out of toddlerhood, he became even more like Roy. This tweaked and delighted us at the same time. Others would notice, too. Often, they quickly brushed it aside, pointing out how the boys were two totally different people. Clearly this was true, but what they were really saying was we shouldn't confer anything from "the dead" on to the living child. Well, I'm not afraid of "the dead." In fact, "the dead" is my son, too. It's also my father, for that matter.

Happily, we went on to have *another* child. A fifth child we never would have had if not for the death of our third. Sound familiar, like history repeating itself? I know we often end up like our mothers, but this is ridiculous. I didn't think I could have another girl after three boys in a row, but here she was. Another gift from God. Strangers would comment how we had the "perfect" family, two boys and two girls. Not exactly perfect, but we had undergone a soul perfecting, or is it correcting? Those images of perfection will get you every time. It's what keeps the Tragedy Club members so isolated. Everybody thinks everyone else is having the perfect life. I guess I'm guilty of it, too, because I never correct strangers about thinking that we have the perfect family. But, it's only because I don't want to ruin their day.

This new baby gave us great joy. She really was a wonderful addition to our family. I remember when I first lost Roy, some people said we should have another child. I thought that's such simple thinking, the idea that he could just be replaced. In fact, that is impossible, even if it was one's aim. Even if he could be cloned, the person we knew would still be gone. A clone wouldn't replace him any more than an identical twin can replace her twin. They are two different people on the inside. That variation in twins' personalities is due to two different souls enlivening two bodies that are genetically identical. Parents are usually aware of a unique bond they have with each child that has a quality all of it's own. The bond is a reflection of the connection between souls that once lost to death, cannot be regained in having another child.

Thus, a new life does not replace the one that is gone. What it does is establish a new love relationship and effect a healing in spite of yourself. The power of such a positive move toward healing cannot be overemphasized. The child surely benefits from all the love that comes her way as it seeps out of multiple broken hearts in the family. The same love and healing would result from adopting a child. Becoming newly active in the life of a child who needs you is very rewarding. It took me a while to learn all of this myself. I remember receiving a condolence letter from a woman saying my comfort would come from my other children. I thought, "How dare she?" until I saw the signature and realized that this woman had lost a child years ago. Then I thought, "Maybe it will." And it certainly has.

So, not all is bleak. My program kicked in while I was in my early thirties and I found out one of my life lessons had to do with judgmentalism and compassion. I became one of the humbled members of the Tragedy Club, but maybe I'll be able to help others emerge from tragic circumstances by highlighting a tangible afterlife and an involved God. He is a Creator who has placed His divine spark in each of us, making us capable of great things. I'm one who believes He has a plan for each of us and that every element of life, even suffering and loss, has a purpose. Near-death experiences go a long way in elucidating these ideas. I don't know how skeptics doubt the truth of these experiences when numerous blind people, sightless from birth, have reported being able to see or "perceive from a distance" during their NDEs. This really supports the idea of an indestructible energy or spiritual element to our being that is unaffected by the frailties of the physical body. Blind individuals must be here to learn from the limits of their bodies.

The idea of learning through earthly limitations was once unthinkable to me. George Anderson was quoted in *We Don't Die* as saying, "As I've been told from the other side—although I sometimes find it hard to believe—there are no accidents of the universe. Everything has a purpose, a mission, a meaning. And for the parent who loses a child tragically in an accident, the child was fulfilling his or her mission; the parent was fulfilling that mission too. The parents are in that circumstance to learn a lesson. Maybe the lesson was patience, love, acceptance, understanding, comfort of others. It can be a number of things." Upon first reading that, I thought if I could be convinced that message truly came from Spirit and was accurate, it would completely change the way I viewed our tragedy and life in general. Since my daughter told me she was aware of spirits, I reasoned George Anderson might be doing exactly what he said he was. I thought how great it would be to have a reading with him, but it must be impossible to reach a world famous medium and even harder to get an appointment.

One evening, my sister told me about a meeting she had had that day. The woman that she had met with wore a simple but beautiful necklace, and my sister had complimented her on it. The woman told my sister that it was purchased at a jewelry store we'd never been to. Days passed, and my sister got it in her head that she must get one of those necklaces. Well, we went to that store and while there, a long conversation with a salesperson ensued which touched on loss and grief. My sister mentioned George Anderson and, surprisingly, the salesperson had heard of him. In fact, she had met him before and had his phone number! Needless to say, I soon had the number with instructions to call between certain hours on Tuesdays only. A week later, my husband asked me about all of this, while we were out doing errands. I told him we should consider meeting with George Anderson. He asked what day we were supposed to call and I answered "Tuesday." He wondered aloud, "What's today?" I thought about it and said, "Tuesday." He then asked, "What time are calls taken?" I answered, "Between four-thirty and six- or seven-thirty." We gazed at our watches and noticed it was 4:20 p.m. We then looked at each other and went straight home. I guess it was meant to be. Despite hearing of the extreme difficulty others had of getting through, I reached George Anderson's scheduler that day and the rest is history.

The reading, or discernment, was interesting for several reasons. George is very down to earth and extremely humble in light of how sought after he is. We expected to hear names of a few deceased family members mentioned, but not as many as he came up with, nor were we expecting to hear from *those* individuals. We were seated in a group of about twenty-five people. Our turn would begin when a family member's name was called out and we, as the correct party, took it or claimed it as our possible connection. He mentioned a silly nickname that I called my son and I didn't raise my hand. Another person present tried to take it, but it went nowhere. George then called out a different nickname we used and this time I raised my hand because, well, what was the likelihood of two of my son's nicknames being called out in a row? The reading was a success. The most convincing part was when one relative, who suffered heart and lung problems, said it was the loss of his eyesight that bothered him the most. He even mentioned how one eye was much worse than the other. This blindness was known to no one outside the family and it was what bothered him most. For George to be telling us this was incredible, a direct hit. Occasionally, I tried to validate something like a great-uncle Sam, but George would insist it was directed at my husband, thereby not taking the credit he easily could have. It turned out, much to my surprise, that my husband also had a great-uncle Sam, with whom he was a lot closer than I was with mine. The other convincing element was the way George quoted my father. He didn't just mention that he spoke some Yiddish, but used his exact Yiddish expressions. Not only that, my father repeatedly used his favorite swear words causing George to keep saying "you know what" as in "crock of you know what" and "full of you know what." A skeptic could say those are good guesses, but my husband's family used different Yiddish expressions and he got those right, too, when he was supposedly talking to them.

I was most astounded by something else. I'd been harboring an unusual concern about my son which I had shared with no one, not even my husband. Without being told a thing, George brought it up himself, again and again. It seems my loved ones wanted this issue settled. No cute skeptic is going to tell me this was guesswork based on a general concern a bereaved mother might have. In all the books I read about George Anderson, which contained transcripts from numerous readings he's done, nothing like what he said to me was ever said to another parent or anyone else for that matter.

There's a common misconception that only the gullible would believe in mediumship. It actually takes enormous sophistication for educated, concrete thinkers to open their minds, look at the content of a number of remarkable readings, and conclude there's something to this. Incorporating this new element into one's belief system takes even more courage. A weaker individual wouldn't try, but instead would cling to previously held beliefs. I'm not saying there aren't psychic frauds. There are fraudulent practitioners of every discipline and particularly in the area of psychic phenomena because of its intangible nature. However, a little critical thinking must be applied here. Just because fifteen different street vendors each try to sell you a fake gold watch, it doesn't mean no real gold watches exist. This is not to say everyone who's grieving should go find a psychic or medium. It is, however, a consideration for those having a particularly tough time. If you've heard, read about, or perhaps seen a talented medium on television, go through the necessary steps to get an appointment. You may have to wait six months or even two years. Put yourself on that waiting list. Grieving is a long process and you can benefit from a discernment at a later point in time as well. Bereavement groups such as the Compassionate Friends may aid you in this area.

To be honest, nothing gave me more comfort or peace than George Anderson's discernment. After the reading, I felt elated. An emotional down then followed, after which my mood evened out. Despite this, I had no regrets because I was clearly better off. In fact, we were permitted to tape the session, and the transcript I made from the tape has served as a continual source of comfort and inspiration. It's funny, but some things he told us about our future seemed extremely unlikely, but have since come to pass.

It's important to remember that grief *is* a process. You

may not have consciously opted for your program, but once in it, there is no choice but to work through it. You're operating out of the limited perspective of the difficult moment. It's hard to see beyond it to the big picture which does make sense. Try to have faith to believe this is so, and that there is a purpose to your suffering.

Doing what is necessary, whether it's therapy, group meetings, a grief chat room on your computer, journal writing, exercise, or even short term antidepressants, is work that must be done to bring you toward the goal of healing with as much of your life as possible remaining intact. Try not to engage in destructive behavior. Destructive pitfalls of all sorts loom and must be avoided as you work to maintain a firm grip. You've already taken the hit, now make the loss meaningful by overcoming. Make the effort to be the best self you can muster and let something good come out of something bad.

It may sound unreasonable, but once I had dealt with the grief to a large degree, I didn't want to deal with any later problems. I felt I had had enough. But, I came to accept hardships, annoyances, and the occasional inundation because this is life after all. It's full of these, but it's how you look at them. You do what you have to do, but you need not overreact or let insignificant things get to you, because they don't warrant it. When things go wrong for the people you love, you'll no doubt be dismayed. Just do your best in handling it, and remember, there are things beyond your control. These are the big and small trials and tribulations of your life. We're here to face obstacles from which we gain insight and mellow. Into every life some rain must fall. Sometimes a lot. Every person is affected.

Knowing you've overcome your trial and become an improved human being is your reward. If nothing else, you did what you came here to do. For me, the reward was peace. It came into my life, and everything was somehow changed for the better. It's funny. It was so long since I felt peaceful that I didn't realize how the quality of my life suffered without it. This new contentment came from being relieved of the pedestal, becoming more myself, and finding my spirituality. While the feeling of suspended animation from the shock of the loss has subsided, there remains a residual buffer between me and the rest of the world. It's sort of a safe distance. Viewing my life as an observer as well as a participant means my mood is less controlled by the day's events. Like everything else, my newfound peace does not come easily. It is something I have to work to maintain. It takes three things: daily exercise to aid the body and even the mood, prayer, which acts as a mental cleansing, and reflection to continually evaluate my experience and stay on track. The good news is I'm finally comfortable with my life. I trust in God that it will unfold as intended. I plan to live it honorably, but if I fall short, that's O.K., too.

I hope I've helped my fellow Tragedy Club members in some way, however small, to handle their devastation. In any event, I truly wish you peace, but not good luck because I don't believe in luck. I believe in God.

DISCOVER HOW THE EDGAR CAYCE MATERIAL CAN HELP YOU!

The Association for Research and Enlightenment, Inc. (A.R.E.®), was founded in 1931 by Edgar Cayce. Its international headquarters are in Virginia Beach, Virginia, where thousands of visitors come year-round. Many more are helped and inspired by A.R.E.'s local activities in their own hometowns or by contact via mail (and now the Internet!) with A.R.E. headquarters.

People from all walks of life, all around the world, have discovered meaningful and life-transforming insights in the A.R.E. programs and materials, which focus on such areas as personal spirituality, holistic health, dreams, family life, finding your best vocation, reincarnation, ESP, meditation, and soul growth in small-group settings. Call us today at our toll-free number:

1-800-333-4499

or

Explore our electronic visitors center on the Internet: **http://www.edgarcayce.org.**

We'll be happy to tell you more about how the work of the A.R.E. can help you!

A.R.E.
215 67th Street
Virginia Beach, VA 23451-2061